Just in Time

TRACY MORRISEY

This book is a work of non-fiction. Unless otherwise noted, the author and the publisher make no explicit guarantees as to the accuracy of the information contained in this book and in some cases, names of people and places have been altered to protect their privacy.

WestBow Press books may be ordered through booksellers or by contacting:

WestBow Press
A Division of Thomas Nelson & Zondervan
1663 Liberty Drive
Bloomington, IN 47403
www.westbowpress.com
1 (866) 928-1240

ISBN: 978-1-4908-7464-7 (sc)
ISBN: 978-1-4908-7465-4 (hc)
ISBN: 978-1-4908-7463-0 (e)

Library of Congress Control Number: 2015904715

Print information available on the last page.

WestBow Press rev. date: 4/9/2015

"My grace is sufficient for you,
For my power is made perfect in weakness."

---Christ the Lord

Contents

Contents

Preface

The most peaceful time of the day is when I'm rocking my daughter, Tori, to sleep at night. We pray together, and once she falls asleep, I have my personal time with the Lord. This is a time when my mind is clear, and all I want to do is hear from God. One night in January 2014, I was praying silently and asking for guidance – guidance for my life – guidance in serving the Lord. My heart was heavy and I needed a word from him.

Just a month before, my daddy passed away. He struggled all of his life with addiction and the problems it created. He ran from the Lord and alienated his family. My relationship with him was a major struggle, yet it still existed. The night he died, December 22, 2013, God intervened in a miraculous way, making known his powerful mercy and grace.

On that January night, as I prayed, God answered. God spoke into my spirit that he wanted me to share the story – the story of my daddy's struggles – through my eyes. He wanted me to share it in a book, and I immediately said, "I don't have time to write a book! I don't know how!" I wondered, did I imagine this or was it the Holy Spirit? I cannot explain how I felt at that moment. My mind was flooded with ideas. I trembled with excitement and nervousness. I wept! Even though my mind had doubt, my body felt the Spirit of the Lord.

You know, we as humans, always expect God to speak to us verbally, but most times, he just puts a feeling in our hearts or a thought in our minds. Many times we shrug it off as a crazy idea, but if we'd go a step further to pray and ask God if it was him, he would let us know.

I prayed and I prayed fervently. I actually prayed all throughout the day and night, "Lord, if that was you, please let me know!" The following night, in my quiet room with Tori, the Lord confirmed his presence. He gave me the title of the book, *Just in Time*. I immediately wanted to add more to the title, like *Just in Time, God's Grace* or *God's Grace Came Just in Time*, but the Lord cut me off and told me simply, *Just in Time*. He told me the book would explain it all. It would explain what came *just in time*. I was so excited the next few days. I felt closer to the Lord than ever! I have always wanted the Lord to speak to me, and I always wondered if I would actually hear his voice. Finally I realized he didn't have to be audible to be speaking to me. It was an amazing feeling!

God instructed this book to be written for two reasons. He wants it to help those who struggle to love and respect their parent or loved one in spite of addictions. He wants people to know, through prayer and faith, he will grant his grace when you least expect it. He will give it to the ones who seem least deserving.

I dedicate this book to my daddy, Robert Van Nichols. I know that his soul is in heaven, and I thank God for directing each step on December 22, 2013 to allow for his salvation. Not all of us will be so fortunate. Don't chance it! Give your life to Christ sooner rather than later!

through prayer and faith, he will grant his grace when you least expect it. He will give it to the ones who seem least deserving.

I dedicate this book to my daddy, Robert Van Nichols. I know that his soul is in heaven, and I thank God for directing each step on December 22, 2013 to allow for his salvation. Not all of us will be so fortunate. Don't chance it! Give your life to Christ sooner rather than later!

Beginning of the End

On December 22, 2013, I woke up to a sunlit Sunday morning, eager to go to church. I was extra excited because it was close to Christmas, and my family was having dinner at my mom's that afternoon to celebrate. Around 12:30 p.m. as I was leaving church, Daddy crossed my mind. I called him, and he answered sounding like he always did – bored and lonely. I asked him how he was doing, and he said, "Fine. Just came in from sitting outside." It was warm that day. He liked sitting outside in this old, white, plastic chair, smoking cigarettes and drinking beer. He talked to neighbors – or himself, if no one was around. He'd sit in that chair for hours.

I told him I was just calling to check on him. He asked me to come see him sometime, as he always did. "Kiss that baby girl for me," he said, referring to my daughter, Tori. He was in a decent mood and didn't ask for anything. He just listened and talked, without an agenda. It was nice, but unusual. I told him I'd visit soon and would kiss Tori for him. Then we hung up.

My phone rang again around 6:30 that night. It was him. I was actually surprised that it took so long. One phone call always prompted another. We could never just have a nice conversation. It was always followed by another call where he needed something or had a problem. This time was no different.

When I answered, he was gasping for breath. "Tracy, something is wrong." I wasn't alarmed at first because many of his phone calls started this way. He went on to say he thought he may have had a heart attack but was unsure. His next words startled me. "Tracy, blood is everywhere. I threw up blood all over the floor, and it looks like chunks of my liver are in it." I immediately asked if he had been drinking alcohol, and he replied, "No, not for three days." Then I thought maybe it was something he had eaten but he denied that as well. So many times, a phone call like this was a cry for attention and rarely ended up being true. Nevertheless, he asked me to call 911.

My sister, Erin, and my mama had been listening to the conversation. I told them everything, and we all thought it was a ploy for attention. He was probably out of food and money. Still, something didn't feel right in my spirit, so I called him right back to see if his story had changed. He was still gasping and told me it wasn't a heart attack, but something was very wrong. He had been sitting back, watching television and feeling fine. When he stood up, he got extremely dizzy and threw up blood everywhere. He kept reiterating how blood was everywhere. I believed him. I told him stay calm, and I would call 911.

I made the call, gave them the address and situation, and they assured me they were on the way. In my mind, he was fine, probably exaggerating. I called his house a little later, and when there was no answer, I knew the paramedics had him. My plan was to call the hospital in about an hour to talk with him and find out what was wrong. I had done this many times before, but tonight would be different.

Where He Came From

Robert Van Nichols, my daddy, was born in June 1948. Everybody called him Van. He was the oldest of four children. He had two brothers and a sister. He spent the majority of his childhood in the small town of Bell Arthur, North Carolina, in the country. He grew up on a dirt path that is now paved and called Nichols Road. Most of his family lived on that road or in the surrounding area.

Growing up in the country, of course, Daddy was a country boy. Family members always told me Daddy was spoiled rotten as a child. He was a very handsome young fella. They say he had lots of friends and was well-liked. He loved the outdoors and did many of the things little boys his age did.

My daddy, Van, when he was eighteen months old

His upbringing was another story, though. Daddy's parents, Granddaddy Bob and Grandma Chris, were a very handsome couple when they first married. I was told they were very much in love initially. Unfortunately, Granddaddy Bob fell into the arms of alcoholism. Alcoholism plagued the Nichols family. Granddaddy Bob's generation was affected, and it was passed down to my daddy's generation. My cousins and I always called it the "Nichols plague" or the "generational curse." Either way, it was devastating and left a permanent mark on so many lives.

Granddaddy Bob was verbally and physically abusive at times. There was also talk of infidelity. Daddy never spoke to me a great deal about his daddy and their relationship, but when he did, the stories were harsh. Daddy always described him as a "mean drunk." The one story that stands out in my mind is an argument that occurred at the kitchen table when Granddaddy Bob chased my daddy around the table with a knife. I think there were many other occurrences like this, but they were never spoken of to me. I witnessed their relationship as I grew older, and it was never what you would call normal.

Granddaddy Bob

Grandma Chris was a working mother. She was a hairdresser. She was a beautiful lady, always well dressed, with her hair done perfectly. She was mild mannered, quiet, and very reserved. She did her best to care for her family. She withstood many years of turmoil with Granddaddy Bob. Whether inherited or learned, Grandma Chris struggled with showing love and affection. Daddy spoke of this many times, and I experienced it first-hand as I grew to know her. Daddy's siblings also felt the absence of that love. I think they all strived to earn her love but felt they never did.

Grandma Chris holding me, 1974

When talking about his childhood, Daddy rarely spoke of good times when it came to his parents. His stories of good times, loving times, always involved Granddaddy and Grandmama Nichols. They were Granddaddy Bob's parents and lived on that same dirt path in Bell Arthur. I'm sure their home was Daddy's refuge from the torment he experienced in his home. Daddy looked to his grandparents for what he couldn't get from his parents. My daddy always credited them with raising him. He spent much of his time with them and moved into their home for good when he turned sixteen. By then, Granddaddy Bob and Grandma Chris were headed toward divorce.

Daddy was the firstborn and the apple of Granddaddy and Grandmama Nicholses' eyes. They loved him dearly, and there was nothing they wouldn't do for him. They showered him with love and material things. At sixteen, he had a brand-new car.

When Daddy spoke of Granddaddy and Grandmama Nichols, he spoke of them with love. Thankfully, I experienced that love, also. I can remember spending time with Granddaddy Nichols. He carried me around in his arms, smoking his cigar. He made me feel like a queen. I always felt so proud. There wasn't anything he wouldn't buy for me down at that local store in Bell Arthur. My fondest memory was how he used to make me grilled cheese sandwiches. The cheese just oozed out the sides of the bread. Nothing big, just the small things filled with love that I remember and treasure the most.

Granddaddy and Grandmama Nichols

Grandma Nichols was the best. I spent many weekends with her, and we always went to her house on Thanksgiving and Christmas. She was always cooking and was the best at it. She collected porcelain dolls. I remember she had one room dedicated for all those dolls. She'd always let me play with them. Almost every weekend she played dominoes or rummy with other family members. I sat and watched her. I was content just being in her presence. She always attended church and sang in the choir. She was a God-fearing Christian and probably the person who introduced my daddy to the Lord. There was a lot of love in Grandma and Granddaddy's house, so I know exactly the kind of love he received from them. When he was a youngster, I am sure Daddy was drawn to the many material things he was given, too.

Daddy's childhood had its ups and downs. His parents went through many struggles that trickled down into the lives of their children. They didn't give Daddy the love he needed and couldn't always provide the material things he wanted. There was abuse, fighting, alcohol, and adultery. Daddy had an outlet, though, to escape the torment going on at home. His grandparents tried to fill the void and provide for his every need. Sometimes, I think their best intentions to do well by him affected Daddy negatively as he grew into a man.

Daddy, unfortunately, was left scarred from all this. His siblings were too. Some of them didn't have a place to get away from it all. The curse – the plague – would get them all, even my daddy. He would become an alcoholic, an abuser, and an adulterer. He would struggle with showing love and become materialistic. He would struggle with depression and become self-destructive. He would have everything and end up with nothing. He would lose the will to be better, the will to be a father, a grandfather – the will to overcome. Ironically, Daddy always vowed he would never be like his daddy.

They Meet – They Marry – A Child is Born

When Daddy was younger, in his teens and early twenties, he was so handsome. He was a sharp dresser with a smile that brightened any room. He was always a charmer, even until the end of his life. Wherever he was, he was the center of attention. He had a big presence to be such a little man. He flirted with every woman around, whether they reciprocated it or not. He stole my mama's heart with that charm and smile. He practically stole her soul.

My handsome daddy when he was in high school

They met at the local bowling alley. She was a junior in high school. Her name was Linda Louise Mills, my mama! She was a young, beautiful woman with long, brown hair. She lived in a nearby town, Ayden, North Carolina. She came from a great family. Mama was the baby of the family with two older brothers and a sister who passed away at an early age. Their mama, Granny, raised them alone. Their daddy was an alcoholic and never around. They struggled financially but always knew the value of family.

Mama was a good girl, and she caught my daddy's eye. Likewise, she was drawn to him. He showed interest, but unfortunately, he showed interest to many women. They dated for several years but nothing was easy. Many times Mama tried to move on. Mama attempted to date other guys but Daddy would always throw a monkey wrench in her efforts. She had a date with another guy one night and Daddy, being the slickster that he was, came to her house that night. He knew about the date and supposedly wanted to help her get ready for it. His tactics worked every time. This other guy, who was always on time, courteous and treated Mama like a queen, just couldn't hold a candle to my daddy. Daddy was always late, if he even showed up, and Mama always had to fight for his affection. What is it with us ladies?! We always reject the good ones. We die to have the ones that treat us badly, cheat on us and make us miserable. That was Mama and Daddy!

As I've mentioned, Daddy was used to having the finer things in life. He had the new car, of course, and appearance was everything to him… then, and throughout his life. He always exaggerated the cost of things. If something was $100, he'd tell people it was $300. Mama, on the other hand, didn't come from money. Mama told me how she bought Daddy a nice coat one Christmas. She got it on sale, which was the only way she could afford it. She and Daddy went out with friends shortly after she gave him the coat, and he bragged to them about the cost of it. Mama said he told them the regular price of the coat instead of the sale price. I laugh at this because Daddy did this all throughout his life. I didn't realize it started at such an early age.

Mama hung in there, even though she knew there were other women. She continued to fight for his love, his attention, him! It was a struggle...always a struggle. One day, a friend of Mama's called to inform her that she was moving to Virginia and wanted Mama to come along. She gave it serious thought but knew she never would. As a desperation move, Mama told Daddy she was going to move with her friend. It worked. Shortly after, Daddy agreed to marry Mama. They were twenty years old and were married on November 30, 1968.

Van and Linda, my daddy and mama, in their early twenties

Daddy drank alcohol and smoked cigarettes when they met. At the time, I don't think Mama knew it would be an issue. She could deal with it then. The cheating was her major concern, and marriage didn't fix their problems. The drinking would soon worsen, and the violent behavior would start. He began gambling, sometimes losing all of their money.

My mama endured over twenty-three years of heartache, disappointment and torment. On the other hand, she felt some of the deepest love and had some of the best times with the same man that caused all of that pain. She produced two children with him that she loves to the moon and back. I can say that Mama stood by my daddy's side through some dark times. She forgave the unforgivable. She made him better. This is one woman that had unconditional love mastered, but there was a price.

You will read about some of Mama's struggles with Daddy in this book, but I want everyone to know this! My mama, his only wife, was the love of his life. He regretted everything he ever did to her. I think, sometimes, in that crazy mind of his, he thought he could get her back. I've learned throughout life that the people we love the most are the ones we hurt the most. What kind of sense does that make?

LIFE GOES ON

Life went on for Mama and Daddy. Married life for Daddy was not well-received. It was much different from his single, carefree life where his family helped provide for his needs. He had to take the reins now, but would he? When Daddy decided to marry Mama, his family wasn't very pleased. Mama believes it was because her family was poor. Daddy's car was taken away from him, but they were allowed to live in a camper in Bell Arthur. Unfortunately, the camper caught on fire one night, and they had to move. They rented a small trailer in Shady Knoll Trailer Park in Greenville. Before long, Daddy lost his job, and they moved back to Bell Arthur.

While staying with family in Bell Arthur, Daddy reunited with an old girlfriend. Mama got word of it from the girl's brother. Daddy and the other woman wanted to be together, but her father wouldn't allow it. The woman's father threatened to disown her, and I guess that was enough to keep them apart. Feeling rejected, Daddy came home to Mama and recommended they buy a trailer and move. She knew why, and she was heartbroken. She moved with him just the same.

I think he was working again at this time. He worked for a tobacco company, something all of his family was involved in. Mama had gone to a two-year business college and was working for the state. They struggled financially, but nonetheless, they were off to Shady Knoll Trailer Park with their new trailer.

What a roller coaster ride! When would they get a break? Not anytime soon because shortly after all of this, Mama got pregnant with me! I was born in June 1972, Tracy Lynn Nichols.

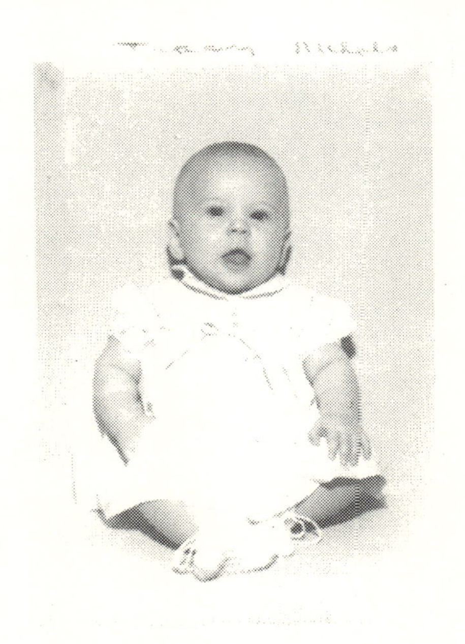

Tracy Lynn Nichols, 1972
"Used with permission. © Lifetouch Inc."

Mama was elated and overwhelmed at the same time. Daddy was being Daddy. He actually almost missed my birth. God only knows what he was doing, but Mama thinks he was playing poker – gambling. Times were hard for Mama. She was alone most of the time and caring for a baby. Thank goodness for her family. Mama told me of a time when I was only a few months old. It was winter. Snow was on the ground, and Mama didn't have any milk. She sent Daddy out to get milk and bread. He returned TWO DAYS later. No explanation, no nothing! My uncle came out in the bad weather and brought us what we needed. This was one of many occurrences that took place throughout the years.

Memories at Quail Ridge

When I was almost two years old, Mama and Daddy decided to move our trailer to a new development. We moved to Quail Ridge Trailer Park on the Belvoir Highway. This is where some of the best and worst times of my life took place, but wow...how I loved this place! I remember so many details about it. We were on Lot 27, and I can even remember my phone number from back then. I thought our trailer was awesome. We had neighbors all around with other kids my age. Some of my best friends in the world lived beside me. Liz and Nickie were my two best girlfriends. We were all close. We played together. Everybody knew everybody, and we all kept our doors unlocked. It was safe. It was commonplace to hear the laughter of children on a daily basis. My childhood, for the most part, was awesome. It was just like any other child's life when it came to my neighborhood, my friends, and my activities.

Daddy, Mama and me in front of our trailer in Quail Ridge, 1974

I remember playing outside in the summer until Mama called me in for supper. I woke up on Christmas morning every year with everything I ever wanted lying in my living room floor. I had wonderful birthday parties with all of my closest friends and relatives. I loved the school I attended. I was athletic, pretty much a tomboy. My mama and I (and sometimes Daddy) regularly attended Bell Arthur Christian Church where I was part of the youth program. That would be where my spiritual foundation was laid. We had a pool, a trampoline, and an Atari (that's a 1980's version of a Play Station, ha-ha). I had a nice bike, and we even had ponies at one point. We were a low-middle class family, but I thought we were rich. We looked like a very functional family.

Not only were the children in my neighborhood close, but the parents were pretty close as well. Almost every couple in the neighborhood had a shed in the backyard, where parties and get-togethers took place every weekend. It got pretty rowdy once in a while. Drinking alcohol was a pastime norm, and it wasn't surprising when a fight broke out. While the parties were going on, the kids were usually away doing "kid stuff," but we always heard the stories when we got home. I remember Mama telling me about the lawn mower competition. Daddy had a riding lawn mower, and, of course, so did several other men in the neighborhood. One night after hours of partying in the backyard, they all got into a debate about whose lawn mower was the fastest. So to decide, in the middle of the night – in their drunken stupor – they raced lawn mowers. I can't remember who won but if it wasn't my daddy, then the others somehow cheated. Seems harmless and fun, right? Well, it seemed that way.

We lived in Quail Ridge until I was fifteen, and during that time I saw things change and some things stay the same. Some of the families in the trailer park withstood the test of time, while others didn't fare so well. Some committed adultery and divorced. Some died from alcohol abuse. Some are still married to this day. Nevertheless, I loved those families and all my friends. They hold a special place in my heart, and I will always cherish my memories there.

Our beautiful home in Quail Ridge

I didn't just witness the life of others, though. My own family was going through its own dilemmas. While there were so many good memories, there were just as many bad. In the open, everything was great. It was home, behind closed doors, where the real terror took place. It was easy to hide from others. Most of the neighbors and most of my friends' parents didn't have a clue what was going on in our home. It wasn't every day. Sometimes, it wasn't every month, but that was the bad part. You never knew when it was coming.

There Was Good in Him

I want to share with you the many good qualities about my daddy, because I have learned there is good in everyone. Despite his alcoholism and other demons he struggled with everyday, there was still good in him. As a child, I seemed to only see the good in my daddy. Even when his actions scared me or his yelling startled me, it was so easy to forget then. It was not until I was older that the bad overshadowed the good, never to leave my memory again.

If I haven't already said it, Daddy was very handsome. I know! I know! I've already said it. He was very particular about everything – his clothes, his hair. Daddy always had his clothes starched and ironed. There was never a hair out of place on his head. He kept his vehicles clean. He took pride in his appearance. His teeth were bright white. He had a beautiful smile. Daddy was very loving at times. As a youngster, he was the center of attention everywhere he went. He was very sociable, and nothing changed once he became my daddy.

Daddy loved to garden. He always grew his own tomatoes, cucumbers, and green onions. I remember he'd cut them up and put them in vinegar with salt and pepper. These were always the key ingredients Daddy put on everything. I grew to love these foods, just as he did. My daddy ate sardines out of a can. We ate Beanie Weenies and Vienna sausage. The list goes on, and they were always topped off with salt, pepper, and vinegar. My daddy ate these things, so I ate these things. I loved my daddy. I was Daddy's little girl. Because of him, I ate a steamed oyster when I was five years old and have loved them ever since.

Daddy also loved to hunt. He hunted rabbit, squirrel, and dove. I think he killed deer sometimes too. I say that because we used to eat deer a lot. We ate everything he brought home. He was a great cook, on the grill or in the kitchen. He even cooked collards, and they were so good. He loved to grill out, but that usually included drinking beer. Whenever Daddy cooked, it was always late at night when we ate. I never knew it took two hours to cook hamburgers and hotdogs on the grill. Beer always prolonged the process. We got used to it. It was the joke of every cookout.

Daddy was also a fisherman. He fished in fresh water and down at the ocean, but freshwater fishing was what he loved most. I always heard about bream, crappie and bass. Again, we always ate what he brought home. He even took me fishing with him on occasion. I loved it! I don't know if he did, though, especially when I got the hook stuck in my cousin's ear. Ouch!

Daddy was crafty. He could build anything. At one point, he built houses for a living. He built a very nice den onto the back of our trailer. The decks and porches for our house were all built by him. The coffee tables, end tables and much of the furniture in our home were built by him. You name it, he could build it.

Daddy building a deck on my eighth birthday

Probably the best attribute Daddy possessed was his ability to sing and play music. I grew up loving Elvis Presley because my daddy loved Elvis. He could sing just like him. Daddy sang country, gospel, everything. He played the guitar and the piano, all by ear. It was amazing to see and hear. I remember weekends in our trailer. The stage was set in the den with guitars, microphones, and "us" singing. I sang with Daddy a lot. Those were good times. He inspired me to sing. I sang in church as early as five and continued through my early teens. I was always excited when he came to watch me. My uncle always said Daddy could've been a country singer if things had been different.

*Daddy and me putting on a concert
when I was four years old*

These were the best things about Daddy. I treasure them and will remember them for the rest of my life. These qualities and the love that came with them are what made it so easy to hope for better from him.

THE FIRST BAD MEMORY

When I was thinking back to the first bad memory – the first memory that terrified me – it came to me in a split second. I will never forget it, yet it is a moment in time that is almost a blur. When I think of it, it is as if I am recollecting a movie I once saw. It doesn't seem real now. I can see my face…the terror, the tears, and the fear.

I was six years old. It happened in the front living room of the trailer at Quail Ridge. Mama and Daddy were arguing. It was deafening. Daddy's cursing could pierce you like a knife. I ran from another room to find Mama sitting in a chair against the back wall crying. Daddy was sitting in the chair directly across from her holding one of his many shotguns. It was aimed at Mama, and it was loaded. He was drunk and threatening to kill her. I jumped on top of Mama, sprawled my arms and legs out wide and tried to cover her body. I was crying and screaming, "Please don't do it." More piercing words were thrown around. We were all crying at one point. By the grace of God, he finally put the gun away, and we soon returned back to normal – our normal.

It wouldn't take me long to forgive and forget – to go on loving my daddy as if nothing had happened. I mean, I was six years old!

Recently I asked Mama if she remembered what triggered him to get so angry and get the gun. She couldn't recall. She said, "It didn't take much to trigger his anger. I could've stayed at the grocery store too long or something crazy like that." Looking back, there never was a substantial reason for arguing. It was just a natural part of my household.

How Did Everything Go Wrong?

Throughout my childhood, there were so many memories – fond ones and scary ones. There were good days that turned into bad nights. As time passed, Daddy's struggles worsened, and I couldn't forgive and forget so easily anymore.

Like I said, I was Daddy's little girl. I kid you not, in my entire childhood, Daddy spanked me one time. It killed him to do it. I remember it like yesterday. We lived in the trailer and had an above-ground pool. It was empty of water, but warm weather was coming. It was full of leaves on one end where a tree stood over it. I decided that I wanted to clean it, so my friend, Nickie, and I proceeded to clean it. The lining of the pool was coming away from the side. I handed her a rake, and I grabbed the hoe. We went at it like we were chopping wood. We were short so we were standing on a table. The first time my hoe went down to grab some leaves, it hit the lining and produced a nice hole. We stopped immediately. I sent Nickie home. We were only eight years old. Of course, I didn't say a word but Daddy had an eagle eye. He saw the hole and came to me immediately. I had been the only one home that day. I started to cry and told him what we had done, but I told him it was Nickie's fault. That wasn't a smart idea because then he wanted to go ask Nickie, who was only two houses down. I was busted! I had to admit I did it. He made me go get a belt. I tried to get a really small belt of Mama's, but I had to get one of his. He made me turn around and bend over. He gave me one lash. It really didn't hurt but I cried because my feelings were hurt. I think he cried too. That is the only time he spanked me, but it definitely wasn't the only time I did wrong.

Mama was the punisher, the spanker, and boy could she deliver! She didn't need a belt! She always used her hand, and it hurt, but I usually deserved it. She also grounded me as part of my punishment. I remember if I didn't get up on Sunday to go to church, she grounded me the next weekend. During this particular time, I went to Sportsworld (a roller skating rink) every weekend with my friends to skate. I loved it. I skated from age eleven to fifteen. If I couldn't go, I thought I would die! Mama always stood her ground. I begged and begged, but she wouldn't budge. Daddy never got involved until I went to him with my lips poked out. "Mama won't let me go to Sportsworld," I said with the saddest little face. He'd always ask what I did wrong, and I'd always downplay it. He'd go to Mama and say, "Let this young'un go to Sportsworld." She looked at me with such an evil eye, but I went. We all do that to our parents, right?

Christmas was usually a very pleasant time for me. Mama might disagree. Many times, Daddy took our Christmas money and lost it gambling, but somehow I never felt the repercussions. Mama always made a way.

I remember Christmas Eve one year when I was ten years old. I was awakened out of a dead sleep, hearing voices outside. It was late, probably 2:00 a.m. It was my daddy and a neighbor putting my trampoline together. Daddy was drunk. I remember laughing and going back to sleep. I just acted surprised the next morning.

Then there was the Christmas Daddy bought two ponies for my sister and me. We named them Fred and Roxie. Can you imagine watching us ride those ponies through the ditches of our trailer park? It was hilarious! We kept them at a stable down the road, rarely rode them and ended up selling them. Unfortunately, Daddy never saw anything too expensive. No matter how unrealistic it may have been to buy or how "in debt" it was going to make us, he dove right in. Everything was always a deal. He could never pass up a deal!

My sister, Erin, on one of the ponies
Daddy bought for Christmas

Just about everyone in our neighborhood owned a boat, and we always went to the river when it was warm. We usually ended up at Whichard's Beach or Seine Beach in Grimesland. For years, we went boat riding with our neighbors, but eventually, we got our own boat…a pontoon boat. I loved it! I remember that before we could go to the river, Daddy would wash it. I'd get so mad because it would take so long. We were putting it in the water anyway. Why wash it first? That was my daddy, though. I think there is a medication for that now.

Our very own pontoon boat

We had the boat for years. Skiing and riding were awesome. Daddy was usually pleasant during the day on the boat, drinking his beer. His beer of choice was Natural Light, and that's what he usually drank. Sometimes, though, he drank liquor and oh man! Liquor made him mean, even meaner than when he drank beer.

More times than none, whenever we left the river to go home, Daddy would do a "Jekyll and Hyde." Mama always drove home because Daddy had been drinking. He always tried to drive but we always said no. He'd say, "I'm not drunk…I'm just drinking." Like clockwork, on the way home, he would start arguing and yelling. One night, I recall him taking his fists and slamming them down on the dashboard over and over. My mama actually had to pull over and calm him down. We knew it would be bad when we got home. We'd be up all night, listening to him argue. We normally just sat or lay in the bed, frightened and listening. He would say over and over how Mama was no good, sorry! He'd go on for hours. Sometimes if we got scared enough, we would try to leave. If he was awake, we couldn't, but if he would pass out, we'd flee to my granny's, always returning the next day.

That is one thing my daddy did well, apologize. Sometimes I didn't want to go back but my Mama always did. She never wanted to lose hope. She wanted to keep the family together. My granny didn't want us to go back either. Granny's prayers probably kept us alive.

Unfortunately, Granny had to endure some of Daddy's wrath. I remember one night at the trailer…I was maybe eight years old. Daddy had been gone. It was so peaceful when he was gone. Granny was spending the night with us. We had a mattress we would put in our back den when I would have friends over. This particular night, Granny, Mama and I were sleeping on that mattress. Daddy came home drunk, and he was ready to argue. He resented my granny. She represented all things good, and she wanted Mama to leave him. I can remember his every step that night. He came in the den and sat on the stool, just over our heads. He started calling Mama names. He'd always ask Granny, "Has she (my mama) told you what she's been doing?" He was inferring that my mama was cheating on him which was not true. He cursed her up and down. When there was nothing else he could say he went to his shotgun case. He loaded it and sat back on that stool at the head of the mattress. He dared us to move. I was shaking like a leaf. He told us he was going to kill us. Somehow, he could say the same things differently over and over. It could extend out for hours. I laid there praying he would get tired and go to sleep. He finally did that night. He got into my bed for whatever reason. He had a cigarette in his hand and fell asleep. He caught the bed on fire and burned his arm pretty bad. It was so scary. I never thought that night would end. We tried to get some sleep. The next day, it was like nothing had happened… to my daddy. Daddy didn't have a problem showing his other side to Granny. I guess he figured she knew already.

The one other time Daddy showed his stripes to Granny was when I was seven. We were going about our day pretty peacefully. I think it was a Saturday. Daddy was drinking and he seemed pretty depressed. I was watching him that day, following him around. I watched him get one of his shotguns. He got the shells and then some string. He kept sitting me down and telling me he loved me. Even at that age, I knew what he was doing. He was getting things together to kill himself or so he wanted me to think. He had a chair out in the backyard. As soon as I figured out what he was doing, I told Mama and Granny. Even with them begging him to stop, he wouldn't. I was holding onto his leg crying, "No, No!" as he tried to walk out the back door. That was so traumatic for me then. I realized, as I got older, my daddy would do drastic things to get attention. That was the case that day. He ended up going inside and passing out. Granny and Mama hid all of his guns, and for the rest of the day, all was peaceful again.

Granny wanted my mama to be happy, but she didn't believe it was going to happen with Daddy. Nevertheless, she tried her best to help with the situation. There was one weekend when Granny wanted to take me to my uncle's house with her to see my cousins. Mainly, she wanted to give Mama and Daddy some time alone. She was hoping this time would give them a chance to talk through things and get their affairs in order. I didn't want to go. I was so afraid of leaving Mama alone with Daddy. I went, but was homesick the entire weekend. That weekend only confirmed that Daddy was never going to change. She told me when I was older that as soon as we left, he told her he was going to make her life miserable that weekend. He practically held her hostage all weekend. He verbally tortured her. He chased her around the house with his machete knife. This was a huge, very sharp knife that he used to skin the animals he hunted and killed. She ran through the house, screaming, fearing for her life. The weekend she had so hoped would be a new starting point for them turned into a nightmare.

My beautiful Granny, Beulah Cannon Mills Haddock, 1977

During this time, Mama and I were inseparable. I never wanted to leave her alone with Daddy. I was her protector, so I thought. When he was gone, we were at peace. Our Friday nights usually consisted of going to West End Circle for dinner. This place had the best cheeseburgers in North Carolina. You'd drive up and the waitress would come to your car. We would order the extra-large cheeseburger and split it. We always got a Pepsi to drink in the glass bottles…the best (I'm telling my age now). Then we'd go home and watch Dukes of Hazzard and Dallas. We popped popcorn and just enjoyed one another. These were such peaceful times and much of the reason I can look back on my childhood with a smile. When the shows were all over and the popcorn was gone, we just sat back and waited…waited for him to come home!

From Weekend Horror to Weekday Torture

Where weekends had been Daddy's time to relentlessly show his other side, weekdays started creeping into the equation. Daddy drank beer almost every day, but he saved the extreme drinking for the weekend, along with the extreme behavior. I guess it was getting harder and harder for him to control. The weekends weren't enough.

I was in middle school. I remember I went to bed early because I had testing at school the next day, CAT testing. I needed to get my sleep and be well-rested. Daddy had been out drinking and doing God knows what. For whatever reason, he always came to my room, no matter what time. This night was no different. He sat beside my bed, placing his hand on my back and calling my name. It was after midnight or later. He wanted to talk. He told me how much he loved me and wanted me to respond back. "I know you love me Daddy, but I've got to get some sleep. I have school tomorrow." He responded, "I might not be here tomorrow." This was disturbing and upset me, but that was the point. I started to cry and hugged his neck, telling him I loved him. He never acknowledged the fact I had school the next day and needed to go back to sleep. He needed this and nothing else mattered. The alcohol caused a total disregard for others' needs. Only his needs were important.

His smell was always the same when he came to my room, smoke and alcohol. He reeked of them both with just a hint of cologne. I hated it! I still do to this very day. That combination of alcohol-and-smoke smell will forever remind me of my alcoholic daddy.

These nightly, weekday visits became more frequent. I came to expect it. The conversation was always the same. "Do you love your daddy?" I'd say, "Yes, Daddy. I'm sleepy, and I have school tomorrow." He talked as long as he wanted, always demanding a response from me, even though I could hardly keep my eyes open. When he was done, he'd get up, walk down the hall to Mama's bedside and proceed to wake her up. Then it would begin – the yelling and the accusations she was "running around" on him. He sat beside the bed, smoking a cigarette and sometimes flicking ashes on her. I'd get up and run down the hall quietly to make sure he wasn't going to hurt her. Most of the time he wouldn't get physical, but the verbal abuse hurt and scared us more than anything physical ever could.

His accusations and behavior made me extremely angry. How dare him! He was the one out drinking at bars without his wedding ring! I guess alcoholics project what they are doing onto their loved ones.

I began getting in bed with Mama when Daddy wasn't there. I guess I was too scared I wouldn't get to her soon enough if I was at the other end of the trailer in my room. He was going to wake me up anyway, so why not bypass him coming to my room. I can remember so vividly the sound of his key unlocking the front door and his footsteps coming down the hall. My heartbeat got faster and louder with every step he took. He would sit beside that bed for what seemed like an eternity. Sometimes, when he couldn't get the rise out of Mama he wanted, he'd get one of his shotguns and sit back down beside the bed. Slowly, he'd put in shotgun shells. With every shell he loaded in the gun, my heart skipped a beat. Once it was fully loaded, I think my heart stopped. I shivered uncontrollably. Would he do it? At that age, I thought he would, especially when he vowed to kill us both.

We dealt with this for years. It seemed to get worse as I got older. The older I grew, the harder it was to forgive and forget.

The Gambling, Money Issues

Daddy loved to gamble, and his favorite game was poker. He always played poker when he went to different clubs or lounges. He really had a problem, but the real problem was when he didn't win. I remember Mama telling me how one year he took her Christmas bonus check, forged her name and lost it all playing poker. My mama was still working at East Carolina University and her salary was minimal. We needed every dime we could get. I don't remember where Daddy worked at that time, but he didn't make enough money to be risking it all by gambling. Not only did he gamble, but he lived like we had all of the money in the world. We didn't! If something was on sale or "a good deal," he could not pass it up, even if we didn't need it. He always had a master plan for making a dollar, but the master plan usually ended up financially breaking him and Mama.

There was the one time where he bought some land in a neighborhood that was being developed. He had big plans for it. I can't remember if he was going to build us a house or build houses to rent out, but neither ever happened. Not only did Mama and

Daddy not have the money to really buy the land, but definitely not the money to do any of the other things Daddy was proposing. He ended up selling the land for less than he paid. He took a loss and so did our family.

Countless Careers

Much like Daddy's dead-end ideas with money, he also had several dead-end jobs. Daddy could've won an award for having the most jobs. First, he worked for a tobacco company early in life. He did that for quite a while. That was probably the most stable job he had. After that, he did everything from selling Electrolux vacuum cleaners to running his own convenience store. He started running a convenience store in a very dangerous part of town. This was one of those big-money dreams. There was an area in the back of the store where he sold hotdogs and other foods. We got a call one day that he was passed out, drunk, back there. I don't think he really ever ran the store – well, actually he did – right into the ground, another financial loss! He worked at Sam & Dave's hamburger joint for a short time. He actually loved this job, and at the time, so did I. He brought me those good cheeseburgers every night he worked. I stayed up until the late hours of the night just to get a hot one. He did work a long spell at Kmart. He worked in appliances as a salesperson. He was good at it, but it would end as well. The last job he had was at the local hospital, in plant operations. He fixed things, built things and painted. These were all things he loved to do. He had great co-workers, good benefits and longevity. However, his lifestyle – his addictions – would end it all. Let me not forget, though, his short-lived career as a cosmetologist.

I will never forget it. Mama was pregnant with my sister, Erin. I was ten years old and in the fifth grade. Daddy decided he was going to quit work and go to cosmetology school full-time in Kinston at Lenoir Community College. He wanted us to move to Bell Arthur into an old house his family owned. This would put us closer to Kinston. So, we rented out the trailer in Quail Ridge and moved everything we had to Bell Arthur. I had to change schools, and I did not transition well. Mama was diagnosed with gestational diabetes. Not only was I crying every day at a new school with lots of strangers, but I had to eat everything baked! Snacks consisted of four pecans, three ounces of grape juice and two carrots. Just kidding, that was Mama's diet. Nevertheless, the change was difficult.

On the other hand, Daddy really enjoyed school. He did well in his classes but you wouldn't know it at home. I remember the night I had a friend stay over with me. I was surprised I asked someone over. The house was so old and had that old smell. There was pink shag carpet in Mama and Daddy's bedroom. My room had flowered wallpaper on the floor. It was hideous! Anyway, after that night I knew my friend Nickie would never spend the night with me again. Daddy came in drunk, arguing. He was really loud. We were peeking around the corner and listening. Mama was very pregnant at this point. I can see it now – he lifted his leg and kicked at her belly. She fell back onto the couch, yelling out in fear. I thought he had kicked her stomach but he just missed. I ran to her, crying. Nickie was terrified. We all were. Those few months were really hard. I became depressed. At the age of ten, I was having thoughts about death, wondering what would happen to me after death. I cried a lot.

I finally went to live with my daddy's sister, Aunt Brenda, so that I could go to my original school. I was with Mama and Daddy on the weekends. I used to have panic attacks in bed at night. I missed Mama so much, and I was worried about her. I wasn't there to protect her. Mama could not stand being away from me either. Finally, Mama and Daddy got the renters out of the trailer, and we moved home. We were so happy. I could smile again, and Mama was able to give birth to Erin with us living at Quail Ridge…home!

My sister, Erin Elizabeth Nichols
"Used with permission. © Lifetouch Inc."

Daddy became a cosmetologist. He worked at a couple of different salons, but was never able to build up a client base. It took him an hour to give a haircut so he couldn't make any money. We used to joke when he cut my hair. I had a short haircut so it shouldn't take him long, right? Well, he combed the back of my neck so much to make sure it was straight that my neck became raw. He was so much of a perfectionist. It was perfect alright. It just took an hour to get it that way. He soon gave up on this profession. Who in his right mind quits his job and moves his family when his wife is pregnant?! My daddy – GOD LOVE HIM!

The Cheating

Mama withstood much more than I would ever know about. As you may recall, Daddy cheated on Mama when they dated and even after they married with the "other woman." After that affair ended, she prayed it was over, but not a chance. Daddy traveled a great deal with his job with the tobacco company. The reality of his cheating became very apparent when he came home with a venereal disease. On weekends Mama and I were left home alone, there were rumors of other women. I remember riding down a nearby road with Mama, seeing Daddy's vehicle at a house we weren't familiar with, only to find out it was the home of a woman he had stayed with all weekend. Mama went home, packed some of his clothes and threw them in the woman's yard. He would soon return home, though, as if nothing had ever happened. Mama always took him back. This would be a recurrent theme all throughout their marriage. I don't know how she did it.

Everyone has their breaking point, though. When I was fourteen years old, Mama had taken all she could. We were still living in the trailer. I was in high school. In a moment of weakness, my mama found refuge in the arms of another man. Regardless of all the accusations from Daddy, Mama had never been unfaithful to Daddy until now. Someone showed her attention – the love she always needed from Daddy – the respect she deserved. Daddy suspected it, but I didn't have a clue. Daddy started investigating, and when he exposed the affair, you would've thought she had done the worst thing ever. At the time, I was devastated. I wasn't so much upset that she had cheated on Daddy. I mean it was commonplace for him to do it, but this was MY mama. It was out of character. I felt like she had cheated on me!

Mama immediately ended the affair, but she and Daddy still separated. Daddy took Mama to court, mainly to drag her name through the mud and humiliate her, but also to decide what to do with Erin and me. Sadly, I had taken my daddy's side because of my anger toward Mama. I still stayed with her most of the time, but I was with Daddy some too. At fourteen, you're so immature. You go where you can get your way, and Daddy let me do whatever I wanted. I took advantage of this. Have mercy! Thank God he had mercy because my daddy would let me take his truck on the weekends and drive without a license. I'd drop Daddy off at a local club and pick him up at 2:00 a.m. How I didn't kill myself or get caught, God only knows. God was truly watching over me because my daddy sure wasn't. I can admit that now but as a teen, it was cool.

Months passed. Daddy dated other women. Mama concentrated on getting her life together and raising us girls. During this time, Daddy begged Mama to come back to him on several occasions but she declined. Mama remembers becoming jealous over one particular woman Daddy was dating. That's all it took. Out of love, but mostly jealousy, she decided to go back.

WHY DID SHE STAY?

There were several times Mama and Daddy split throughout their journey together. She'd leave or she'd make him leave. Either way, it was always short-lived. Mama would give in every time. There was a time when I was nine or ten. Things were really bad at home, and Mama made him leave. He went to Aunt Brenda's house to stay, calling every day to ask if he could come home. She gave a valiant effort the first few times, but finally gave in. I overheard the conversation when she told him he could come home. I was furious and burst into tears. I didn't understand why or how she could do that to me. I was angry with her for days and didn't have much to say to Daddy once he was home.

Daddy was always on his best behavior when he first got home, but in time, he always reverted back to the "Old Van."

I think Mama had that "battered woman" syndrome. She had such a deep-rooted love for my daddy. He had so many good qualities. He had been involved in church at times. He even quit drinking and smoking on numerous occasions. Those times were short and sporadic, at best, but they allowed my mama to hope for better, for change. She had seen him do it, so couldn't he do it again? Unfortunately, these wonderful moments were lost to the addiction my daddy ultimately could not control.

The verbal abuse and the torture had become the norm. It was expected. Even the expectation of it, though, never prepared us for what we got. It never helped take away the fear. Sometimes when you accept this kind of behavior – when you let it become the norm – you forget what normal used to be. You forget that it doesn't have to be this way.

When asked, "Why did you stay?" Mama always said, "I wanted to keep my family together." I didn't believe this answer when I was younger. Now, as an adult, I do! I believe Mama loved Daddy more than I love the Lord. That's a lot. She never gave up – she couldn't. Her hope in his potential won out over losing hope because of his addiction. The bad outweighed the good, but Mama always drew strength and hope from the good times. He always promised he would change. He always said he was sorry. Do you know how easy it is to believe that especially when it is your heart's desire?

A New Home, Hope for a Fresh Start

Mama and Daddy were reunited, and we moved to a brand-new house. I was fifteen, and Erin had just turned five. We had outgrown the trailer, plus Erin needed her own room. The house was just a couple of miles down the road. It was a small, white house with gray shutters. When we speak of it now, we call it the "white house." It had three bedrooms, two bathrooms and a nice yard. It couldn't have been more than 1200 square feet, but we felt like it was a mansion. We were so excited. I think we were all hoping for a fresh start. Maybe a change in address would cause a change in Daddy. Our fingers were crossed.

Our new home, "The White House," with
Mama and Erin out front, 1987

My high school and early college years were spent at the white house. Unfortunately, these years would be more challenging than anything I would ever face. In the past, Daddy's rage and verbal abuse had affected me indirectly, always being directed at Mama. Now, it would also be directed at me. Daddy resented me for always trying to protect Mama.

Our family, 1980s
"Used with permission. © Lifetouch Inc."

We would experience disappointment, DWIs, divorce and death at the white house. The verbal abuse became physical at times. I tried to stay away as much as possible. I was busy with school sports and spending time with friends. I guess I thought Erin could protect Mama now. My anger was at its peak, and I just wanted to be as far away from Daddy as possible.

We have established that Daddy loved to drink, but, unfortunately, he loved to drink and drive. I declare he rarely drove when he was sober! For years, he had recklessly gotten on the roads drunk, but his luck had run out. He seemed to literally get a DWI every time he got on the road. I know he had at least three while we lived at the white house. Lawyers' fees were astronomical, and the financial burden was heavy. Mama struggled, while Daddy never seemed to worry at all. She tried to shield Erin and me from all the stress, but I knew her struggle.

Eventually, the lawyers could only do but so much. On two occasions, Daddy had to go to a satellite jail every other weekend. Those are the weekends I would hang around the house. It was so peaceful. When Sunday afternoon came, we all were sad because he had to come back. What a way to live!

Mama took Daddy back and forth to work every day. He did have a work license at one time but lost that privilege. He lost his license during this time and never had a North Carolina license again.

As if things weren't already bad enough, things worsened for me and Daddy. I was in high school, so of course, I was dating. I'll take part of the blame now, but at the time, I could only feel like the victim.

Mama and Daddy always raised me to treat everyone the same, not to see color. Growing up, I had friends of all races. Having black friends had never been an issue until I started dating one. I knew Mama and Daddy wouldn't approve, even though I didn't think there was anything wrong with it. Nevertheless, I hid the fact that I was dating a black guy. Eventually, they found out and wanted the relationship to end. Unfortunately, it wasn't that easy. I was in love!

In retaliation to my decision to continue the relationship, Daddy vowed to make my life miserable. He insisted I stop playing sports, give up my car and be grounded for life. Mama supported Daddy's decisions to keep the peace. They both handled things differently though. Daddy tried to blatantly hurt me, while Mama wanted me to be happy but worried about my reputation and well-being. I'm sure Daddy had the same concerns but he never came out and said it. He just made life difficult.

Thanks to Mama, I still played sports. After riding the bus for months, I was able to drive my car again, and I was able to leave the house once in a while. Mama paid the price, unfortunately, and so did I. His verbal attacks were very hurtful. He'd say things like, "I'd rather you date a white guy on crack than a black guy." Unfortunately, the actual word he used wasn't so pleasant. He'd wait up for me when I got home from my boyfriend's house. I'd walk into a dark kitchen. He was sitting at the table, drunk. "Where have you been?" he asked. He knew exactly where I had been. I answered, and his next words floored me. He told me he'd rather the police call to say they needed him to come identify my dead body than for me to tell him I had been with my black boyfriend. The topper is when we were all sitting in the living room one night, and Mama picked up my glass of Pepsi to drink some. Daddy said, "You're going to drink after her?" I remember bursting into tears. This would continue for a couple of years.

Looking back, I know my parents wanted the best for me. I can't fault them for being upset. It was hard, socially, dating a black guy. I am a parent now, and I know how it feels to want to protect your child. However, Mama never talked ugly to me. She continued to love me and stood by my side. Daddy didn't handle it as gracefully. His words cut like a knife and left a lasting scar in my heart.

CHRISTMAS OF 1989

The drama continued. It was just before Christmas my senior year in high school. Mama and Daddy had been arguing a great deal. It was a weekend, and I think Daddy stayed drunk from Friday night to Sunday evening. Erin was seven years old. I don't even remember how everything started, but the arguing and threats were so bad we were going to leave. Again, our safe house was at Granny's. The routine was taking all we could take from Daddy, and then attempting to leave. Whenever we'd attempt to leave, he'd always grab Erin and tell us we couldn't take her. She was at that age where she couldn't understand what was going on. She was just scared – scared of Daddy – so she always wanted to go with us.

Daddy was laying back in our blue recliner with Erin in his arms. Mama was in front of the couch, just to his left. She leaned across him to get Erin out of his arms. Erin was reaching for her as well. He proceeded to take his foot and kick her down on the couch. I was standing on his right side, and when this happened, I had a knee-jerk reaction. I lunged forward without even thinking and hit him in the eye with my fist. He was leaned completely back and attempted to jump out of the chair quickly, without success. Mama grabbed Erin out of his arms. His kick wasn't enough to keep her down. Mama yelled, "Run, Tracy, run!" I was so angry and defiant at that time that I said, "I'm not running!" He finally made it up out of the recliner. You have to remember that he was drunk. I was in the kitchen by then, and when he rounded the corner of the kitchen, he swung his fist toward my left temple. Mama was there to grab his arm and lessen the impact of the blow. I was fine but my nerves were all to pieces. Mama, Erin and I ran out the door and got into the GMAC Jimmy truck we had. Daddy followed us to the truck. I was begging Mama to crank the truck and leave, but he was begging us to stay.

The begging continued on both sides for a while, but Daddy won. He went inside, where he passed out. We followed. Erin got in her bed, and Mama and I got in my bed. She slept with me a lot at the white house. This made Daddy mad and was the reason for a lot of late night arguments. He was either drunk or had done something to make Mama angry, so she didn't want to share a bed with him lots of times. No matter what he had done, though, he was the man of the house and she should be in his bed, pleasuring him in whatever way he wanted. Most times, she would rather die than do any of those things.

So that night we slept for a few hours. Daddy was still drunk that morning when he woke up. He started drinking as soon as his feet hit the floor. He decided that day he wanted to wash the house, and he wanted Mama to help him. She had gone to lie in my bed, trying to take a nap. He made his way to my room.

I heard him cursing at her and telling her to get up. I walked back to my room and acted like I was looking in the mirror at something on my face. I was just trying to stay close in case he tried to hurt her. After he finished cursing at Mama, he turned to me and said, "One day I'm going to get you by yourself in this room without your mama around and beat you black and blue. You won't be able to run then." He was referring to the night before when Mama told me to run. I said nothing. He then said, "If you ever hit me again, you'll be sorry." While saying this, he took his pointer finger and pushed me in the forehead, making me stumble backwards. Automatically, without thought, I slapped him in the same eye that I hit him in the night before. Mama jumped up out of the bed and grabbed Daddy. I walked down the hall into the living room and sat in the chair. My nerves were shot, and I was shaking uncontrollably…out of fear, but also out of anger. He stomped down the hallway and stopped in front of the chair I was sitting in. He attempted to kick me in the face. I blocked his foot with my hand. Mama grabbed the phone to call 911 but he snatched the phone out of the wall. This was probably the most physical things had ever gotten. He was yelling how he would love nothing better that to see our bloody corpses laying in the living room floor.

Mama finally got the phone and called 911. Knowing the police were coming, Daddy went next door. By then, Daddy's eye was pretty bruised and swollen. The police finally arrived. They got our story and then went next door to talk to Daddy. The policeman laughed after coming back from talking to Daddy, saying that Daddy looked like the one who got the worst beating. They asked Mama if she wanted to press charges, and she said no. This wasn't the first time we had to call the police, and bless her heart; she could never go through with pressing charges.

My mama was very worried about the tension between Daddy and me. She was worried about my safety. At that time, I was part of a youth group at a Bethel church with several of my classmates. The youth director, Mr. T, and his wife had become like a second mom and dad to me. I was good friends with their daughter. Mama called them and asked if I could stay with them until things settled down with Daddy. So, I spent Christmas with the Tettertons. My mama brought my few gifts there for me to have on Christmas day. I ended up staying there a few weeks. Even though the Tettertons had several children of their own, they opened their home to me and even gave me some gifts on Christmas. The most priceless gift they gave was their love. I will never forget them. I missed Mama so much, and my feelings were so hurt that I wasn't home for Christmas. Finally, Daddy called me after several weeks and asked me to come home. I did. Things were quiet for a while, but only for a while.

I went on to graduate in June of 1990. Nothing changed much with Daddy, but things were never as bad as they were that Christmas. We kept hoping for a change in Daddy. What would it take…a tragedy? We'd soon see.

Uncle Jerry's Suicide

It was July 13, 1990. It was Friday the 13th, so you're always expecting something bad to happen. Well, that's an understatement! My daddy's brother, Uncle Jerry, and his wife, Aunt Teresa, were living in Fayetteville at the time. My Uncle Jerry was in the army. Much like Daddy, he was plagued with the same alcoholism that was so prevalent in his family. He had also been diagnosed with bipolar disorder.

Uncle Jerry, Aunt Teresa, Sherri (oldest daughter) and Kerri (youngest daughter)

I always remember my Uncle Jerry as a happy, loving uncle. When I did get to see him, he was always smiling. My memories of him were fond ones, however, he had struggles. My Aunt Teresa and their two daughters, Sherri and Kerri, endured some of the same experiences my family did. As I said before, the Nichols curse didn't just affect my daddy. It affected all of the siblings.

We got the call sometime before noon. Uncle Jerry had killed himself! He had used a high-powered rifle to self-inflict a gunshot under his chin. We were in shock…devastated, as was his family. We immediately headed to Fayetteville. My daddy was hurt. He didn't want to believe that Uncle Jerry had killed himself. Even on the way there, he talked of different scenarios that could've happened to cause Uncle Jerry's death. Some were so outlandish, and none involved suicide.

It was a hard time for all of the family. Death is always hard, but suicide leaves so many more questions, unanswered questions. Sometimes, tragedies can bring about change in people. I have always believed that God takes us through trials and tribulations for the good of someone. I may not know who that someone is, but I was praying, at this moment, it would be for my daddy's good. I was praying he would change his ways, stop drinking, stop the verbal abuse and start being the husband and daddy we needed. I hoped that somehow Uncle Jerry's death would right Daddy's wrongs.

Unfortunately, Daddy used it as an excuse to get worse. He drank more. He flew off the handle even more than before. I remember months after, in a drunken stupor, he shared his conspiracy theory of how Uncle Jerry had been murdered. Someone crawled in the window and killed him. He really struggled with it. He couldn't let it go. That night, he went to his bedroom. It was very quiet. I followed him and found him under the bed crying, in a fetal position. I got Mama, and we went to him to try to talk to him. He wanted to be left alone and told us so. Of course, we kept trying to comfort him and get him from under the bed. It was cramped under there. All of a sudden, he exploded out from under that bed like the hulk, lifting the box springs and mattress up in the air. He was out of control. We didn't know what to do. We were silenced by this and let him be.

For the next twenty-three years of Daddy's life, July 13th would be a day of mourning for him.

The Separation

Mama and Daddy separated in 1990 and remained separated for a few years. Neither of them wanted to pay for the divorce. Daddy threatened all the time that he was going to take her retirement in the settlement, pretty much taking everything she had. Mama wanted the divorce but she didn't want to lose everything. She was waiting for just the right moment.

While Mama and Daddy were separated, they both enjoyed life. Daddy moved up to our old trailer at Quail Ridge. Mama, Erin and I stayed in the white house. Daddy dated. Some of the women were very nice and good for Daddy. He had a few relationships that even lasted for a few months. He seemed happy, but he was still partying and drinking.

During this time, I was in college. I first went to Mt. Olive College for two years, contemplating pharmacy school, but at the last minute decided to change my major to nursing. I moved home with Mama in 1992 and started attending East Carolina University. I graduated in 1995 and started a nursing job at the local hospital in 1996. Through the end of the nineties, I worked and remained single. Daddy was just down the road and only a phone call away. I kept in contact with him, but I harbored so much resentment toward him. It's strange. Mama found a paper I wrote in college in 1992. It was for my "Marriage and Family" class. We had to write a paper about our family. I don't think my instructor ever expected a paper like this one, but he gave me a good grade nevertheless. I want to share this so you can see just how much resentment I held for my daddy. Right or wrong, the feelings I had for Daddy were disturbing.

The paper was simply entitled, "My Family," written December 1, 1992. It went like this…

When I think about my family, I vision a very long, dark tunnel with a light at the end. My family consists of my mother, my younger sister and me. My parents separated a little over a year ago. I'd like to start my paper by getting the weaknesses out of the way. They are not really weaknesses now, but they are the weaknesses that used to be a part of my family. Thankfully, today, my family has much strength and very few weaknesses.

When my father lived with us, there was a lot of chaos in my household. He was, or should I say, is, an alcoholic. He has been ever since I can remember. When he was around, there was no real stability in the family. One night, everything would be peaceful and the next night would be nothing but arguments. My father was not much of a role model. He played a double role that I could not understand. At times, he wanted to be the boss, and then again, he acted like a child. My mother was the full-time boss, or head of the family. With the circumstances being the way they were, there was not a great deal of love and respect floating around. I held lots of resentment and anger inside of me, just as my mother did. So, it was like my love was overshadowed by the bitterness and, unfortunately, hate. Lastly, there was a lack of trust in my family. Numerous times throughout the twenty- four years my parents were married, my father quit drinking, only to start back in just a matter of weeks. Living on false hopes, my mother stuck with it as long as she could. My dad, along with his alcoholism, broke my family down in all aspects, but the ending is not that bad.

Now that my parents have separated, my new family, with the absence of my dad, is great. There is an atmosphere of peace and tranquility within the family. We look forward to nights shared at home together, whereas before we could not wait to leave home. The trust is overwhelming. My mom and I share this openness that just was not there before. I hear the words, "I love you," a lot more around the house. Everything is so stable. It is as if we have no fears anymore. We feel a sense of security. The burdens we have now, if any, seem very insignificant. My family looks forward to the tomorrows. Before, we used to be under so much stress. We worried all the time. Now, all the stress and all the worries seem to have been lifted. If there is one word I could use to describe my family, it would be unity. We are united in such a way that the bonds of love and security could never be broken. I would not trade anything in the world for my family because it is everything I have ever wanted it to be!

I know some people might be very disturbed about the fact that a family could be better off without the father. I have had several of my family members tell me that my attitude toward my father is not normal. The past would take too long to explain, but a great deal of damage has been done. My mom and other relatives are so forgiving, and sometimes I cannot comprehend that fact. I guess I am not like them. All I know is the facts speak for themselves. My family is a lot better off now than it was before with an alcoholic in it!

I was glad he was gone, but I couldn't let go of the hurt and the pain. I remember how I felt when I saw him with his girlfriend or whoever he was dating at the time. It wasn't jealousy because I definitely didn't want him back with my mama, but I couldn't believe those women couldn't see him for what he was. I knew the dark side of him, but they didn't, yet. I wanted them to know – to know what he had put us through. Daddy could still charm the ladies and show them the fun side of him so many got to see. The ones that hung in there with Daddy for months usually saw the other side, and they ran when they did. Daddy didn't want commitment either, so some left because they wanted a husband. He was not interested.

My graduation picture at East Carolina University, 1995

The Divorce and the Chaos That Followed

In 1993, Daddy took a trip to Mexico and met a woman there. Once he was back at home, he came to Mama and told her to file for the divorce because he was marrying a Mexican woman. He went on to say she could have whatever she wanted in the settlement, and he didn't want her retirement anymore. I would say this was the moment she had been waiting for. She went directly to the lawyer's office and started the proceedings. It all came to an end in 1993.

Needless to say, Daddy did not marry the lady from Mexico. In the following years, meaningless, short-lived relationships characterized Daddy's life. His relationships became fewer and fewer. He started dating numerous women, not the best quality, I might add. He hung out at clubs like a college student. His drinking continued, and his behavior worsened. The decisions he would make in the next ten years of his life would do irreversible damage to his health and his mind. He eventually moved on to harder drugs, and he just allowed everything to spiral out of control.

Daddy took another trip to Mexico. I can't remember who he went with but I know he drove himself. At this point in his life, he had received so many DWIs he would never have a North Carolina license, so he went to Florida some months before and set up residence with some of his Mexican friends. He stayed long enough to get a Florida license so he could drive. He always said he was going to move to Mexico. So, off he went, and this time he stayed for nineteen days. I will always remember the number of days because when he returned home he bragged about being with thirty-eight women, sexually, during that time. He bragged that there was this amazing brothel there in Mexico. This is not something your daughters need or want to hear. I was in my early twenties, and Erin was probably twelve years old. We were at the trailer visiting him. He sat on the back porch and told us he had the big "A." My sister responded, "What?!" I knew what he meant, but I couldn't believe he was saying it in front of my sister. He then said, "I have AIDS." I immediately wanted proof because I didn't believe him. He, of course, argued back and forth with me a bunch of nonsense. I was in nursing school, and I knew how testing for AIDS went. He had no results and no information on treatment. He couldn't tell me where he had the testing done. I knew he was lying and just wanted attention. He was getting it from my sister, a vulnerable child who thought her daddy was going to die. She was in tears, and I was enraged. I tried to console her and reassure her that he was lying, but she wasn't convinced. I don't think we ever spoke of it again. Guess what? He never died of AIDS. He never took HIV drugs. He needed to feel loved. He needed to see our pain in order to believe our love. So unnecessary it seemed, but for him, it was a way of life.

As the nineties continued, things just went downhill for Daddy. The drinking continued, and in the late nineties, Daddy started using drugs – cocaine, crack, marijuana – in addition to the alcohol. We knew because he told us. He bragged about it. We didn't know what to believe but we would soon see the proof.

Daddy decided to move into a camper in his own backyard, while a family of Mexicans moved into the trailer. He said he was helping them out, plus, he didn't need much room. He had it worked out where he could come in and out of the trailer when he wanted. I thought he was crazy, and I told him so numerous times. I would later find out from Daddy's neighbors that he was selling drugs out of the camper.

Even though my daddy drank, did crazy things and made life unbearable at times, this kind of behavior was different. When he came around or called, he was so desperate for money. Daddy was receiving disability now. I really don't know how he was able to get it, but he did. He had chronic back pain, but other than that, he could work! Not working made things worse.

He started wearing gold chains and an earring in his ear which was very unlike my daddy. He was already small in stature and weight, but he looked really thin now. His beautiful teeth were rotting which is when I knew he was doing more than drinking.

During this time, on a July weekend, I got a call from Daddy. I was out of town in Wilmington, North Carolina, so I wasn't close by. He was claiming he had a stroke and heart attack. I didn't believe him at first. You have to understand – my daddy called me all the time with stories, outlandish stories, that weren't true. He cried wolf many times, so I just never knew with him. However, I could tell his speech was slurred, and he complained that his left arm and leg were weak. I told him I was out of town and he would have to call 911. He ended up driving himself to my sister, Erin's, about a mile from his house. She couldn't believe he was able to drive. She and her boyfriend, Jimmy, got him to the hospital. At this time in my life, I had lost all hope that Daddy would ever change. The reality was setting in that I would never have a normal relationship with my daddy.

When I got back the next day, I went to the hospital. I had gotten confirmation from the nurse the night before that Daddy had suffered a mild stroke. She never mentioned a heart attack, but he swears he had one. He was released early that week, and I took him home. His hand was contracted, and he walked with a limp, but it was mild. He was put on blood pressure medicines, aspirin, and who knows what else. It was all in vain. Daddy never took his medicines. He was my most non-compliant patient, by far. His speech was back to normal. On the ride home, he informed me he had been doing cocaine all Friday night and passed out. He joked about it, laughing that when he woke up, he couldn't feel one side of his body. He said he thought to himself, "Those must have been some good drugs – I can't even feel my legs."

That's when he called me. Daddy's blood pressure already ran high. I'm talking 180/100 easy, so there is no telling how high it was from the cocaine. I explained all of this to Daddy and how important it was to stop the drugs and take his medicines. It all fell on deaf ears. He soon stopped doing the hard drugs or used them more intermittently. I don't know how he did it. Even in years past, he could stop drinking or smoking cold turkey and be fine – no detox symptoms, nothing – so much control when it came to some things and so little control when it came to what mattered. This was the first time Daddy had ever been broken by something. My daddy was tough, but the drugs got the best of him. This is when his health, mentally and physically, really began to fail significantly. It was also during this time that Daddy was diagnosed with bipolar disorder. It makes sense… the gambling, the cheating, the erratic behavior, and the major depression. The depression was the worst, though. Alcohol was a depressant, so no matter what medications Daddy took, he never thought they worked. The alcohol always won out, taking away the effects of the medicine.

A Skirt with Death

I guess it was the early 2000s. We always said Daddy had champagne taste and a beer pocketbook. Well, he had bought this old burgundy Cadillac. You would've thought it was the latest model but it wasn't. It was ancient. He drove this Cadillac around without a license, in North Carolina anyway.

Late one night when he was drunk, Daddy ran down in a ditch embankment several times, missed numerous cars and finally ran into a very large, fortunately, forgiving tree. He walked away with a busted lip, another DWI and a driving-without- a-license ticket. Even though he had a Florida license, the police didn't recognize it.

In the middle of the night, I got the phone call to come to the magistrate's office where he was refusing to blow into the breathalyzer. He always refused to blow and swore he wasn't drinking. You could smell the alcohol everywhere plus there were beer cans all in the car. After giving the trooper a very hard time, he was released to me with a court date. I lectured him all the way home and he cursed me in retaliation. He didn't want to hear what I had to say, but I wouldn't stop because I wanted him to know how mad I was. I wanted him to know how irresponsible he had been and how he could've killed someone or himself. I also needed him to know how he had inconvenienced me, but he didn't care. The addiction had his mind, his heart and his soul.

So the Cadillac was out of commission. Over the next year or so, my daddy bought two more cars just like that one for the parts. He took it to an auto garage on Belvoir Highway, paid for the work and never got the car back. What a waste! This was the story of Daddy's life – bad decisions, bad outcomes.

THE YEAR FOR WEDDINGS

In the midst of everything going on with Daddy, my life was still moving forward. It was 2003 now, the year for weddings. After years of being a nurse, I left that career to be a pharmaceutical representative. I was into year two with a great company. My career was stable. I owned my own home and was engaged to be married to my college sweetheart, Dexter Morrisey.

My beautiful sister, Erin, was doing much of the same thing. She had a good job, a nice home and a beautiful son. She was engaged as well to be married to her teenage sweetheart, Jimmy Harris. She was married first, in February. We always joked that she did everything first, even though she was over ten years younger than me. She got married first, had children first – she even gave her life to Christ and got baptized – first! She probably doesn't know this, but she was my inspiration for getting saved.

Daddy gave Erin away at her wedding and put aside drinking for a few brief hours. It was a beautiful wedding, but we were so worried Daddy would come to the wedding drunk. Thank heavens, he didn't.

Erin and Daddy at her wedding, February 2003

Just after Erin's wedding in April, I got married as well. Daddy agreed to give me away too. I got married out of town, so Erin made sure Daddy got to the wedding destination. We all stayed at the hotel where our reception was taking place. Friday night we rehearsed and then the guys went one way – the bar, and the ladies went the other way – to bed.

Dexter and my daddy had a pretty good relationship. Daddy enjoyed hanging out with him and his family. His family all thought my daddy was a hoot and he was, at times. He could make you laugh and cut up with the best of them. He just didn't know when to stop sometimes. The fellas hung out at the bar and then went back to their room to play cards and do what guys do.

The women and I were taking care of last-minute errands. I was very anxious trying to make sure everything was in place for the wedding.

As I lay in bed, I tossed and turned, unable to go to sleep. Erin and I were sharing a room. Daddy and Jimmy would stay in the adjoining room across from us. They hadn't come back yet. I figured they were living it up as long as they could. That is when Jimmy knocked on our door around midnight to let us know Daddy was roaming the halls, drunk. He was being extremely loud and embarrassing, refusing to come back to the room with Jimmy. Jimmy confirmed that Dexter and his family were sleeping.

Great! This was all I needed right now. Daddy eventually came to our door, knocking and hollering loudly to open the door. When I opened that door, I was so angry. He was stumbling. He could hardly stand. He came in slurring his words and saying something about Dexter and those guys having a girl in their room. Jimmy just nodded his head, knowing he was lying. I asked him what he was talking about and he just kept trying to tell me that my fiancé had a girl in his room. He said, "She's in there right now. I'll show you." I called Dexter's room because I wasn't going anywhere. He was sleeping and so were the other guys. Daddy got on the phone with Dexter. Dexter tried to talk him down and convince him to go to bed. When he hung up, I broke down. I yelled at Daddy so loudly and told him I couldn't believe he would allow himself to get so drunk and try to cause unnecessary worry for me on the night before my wedding. I told him that he was NOT giving me away the next day, and if he had transportation right at that moment, I'd make him leave. He dropped his head and eventually went to bed.

Needless to say, I didn't get a wink of sleep that night. Daybreak couldn't come soon enough. I was too stressed to continue to be mad at Daddy. He gave me away as planned and the day turned out great. Even though my daddy had acted so inappropriately, my husband and his family joked about how funny he had been. The irony!

Daddy and me at my wedding, April 2003

Later, at the reception and dance, Daddy stole the show with his charm. He flirted with all the ladies and danced. He was a bit embarrassing but tolerable. All I could do was shake my head, smile and keep on going.

The night before didn't have to happen. It was so hurtful, and I took it personal. I felt he was vindictive. Was it the alcoholism or just him…maybe both? Daddy never apologized, but he did admit he lied. I don't think it ever registered in his mind how that night affected me.

Tragedy on Christmas Eve

Life continued on for us all. Daddy continued to live life on the edge. Would he ever fall over the edge? Time would tell.

December 24, 2006 was the night I just knew Daddy wouldn't make it. This would be the worst accident so far.

Daddy was living with his mama now, Grandma Chris. They lived on Whichard Cherry Road just on the outskirts of Greenville. She had a nice double-wide trailer and Daddy, of course, had his camper parked out back. He owned a van that he was driving with those Florida license. I remember the van was white and had curtains on the windows in the back. It was amazing what he could buy with a disability check. I sometimes wondered if money wasn't coming from another source – selling drugs still.

Grandma Chris had experienced a stroke and after living beside my Aunt Brenda for years, she decided to move. She needed supervision though, and Daddy decided he'd be the one to give it to her. I was concerned that he wasn't the man for the job. He was a stroke victim himself, stayed drunk most of the time, and caused her more worry than anything. I was afraid for Grandma's safety and well-being during this time. Even though her mind wasn't 100 percent after the stroke, she'd tell me on occasion how Daddy scared her sometimes. I knew what she meant. There were many months when I had to help pay the utility bill because Daddy had spent both of their checks. Sadly enough, Daddy had an agenda when he decided to move in with Grandma Chris, financial gain. While Grandma Chris was in the house watching television, Daddy was in the camper playing loud music and getting drunk. Not a good scenario.

On this particular night, Daddy was drunk and had driven down to a local store and juke joint. He was driving back to Grandma Chris's house when he ran off the road into a very deep ditch, hit the embankment and flipped over. He was not wearing a seatbelt. My daddy was found in the passenger side floorboard curled up in a ball, unconscious. He was airlifted to the hospital. My Aunt Brenda went to the scene of the wreck, and the trooper told her Daddy wasn't going to make it.

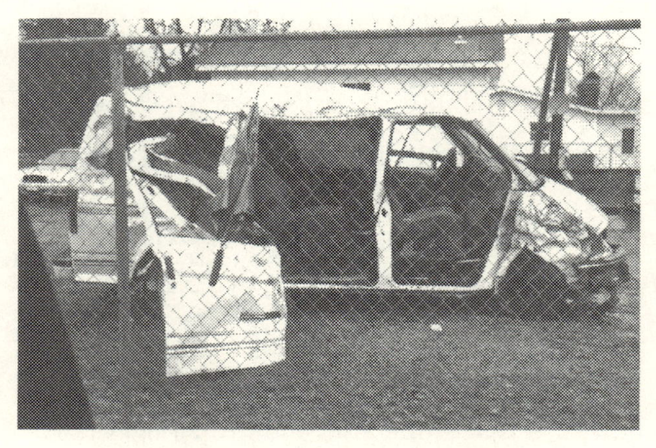

Daddy's van after the wreck, December 2006

Dexter and I were at his parents' house in Faison, North Carolina, about an hour and a half from home. We were opening a few pre-Christmas gifts, when the call came in from Erin. She was crying and told me Daddy had been in an accident. She said, "I think this is it." Dexter could tell from my voice and the conversation that something was wrong. We immediately loaded up and drove back to Greenville.

I entered the hospital room to see my daddy severely swollen and covered in dried blood. Every bone was broken in his face. His right eye and forehead looked like a softball, so bruised. He had broken ribs and a bruised neck. He looked pitiful. He grabbed my hand and tears ran down his face. My sister was very upset. She couldn't stand to see him that way. Neither could I but all I could think was how he had done this to himself. Why hadn't he learned that you can't drink and drive? I prayed because I knew my heart was bitter. His blood alcohol level was through the roof and he had traffic citations waiting for him if he made it out alive.

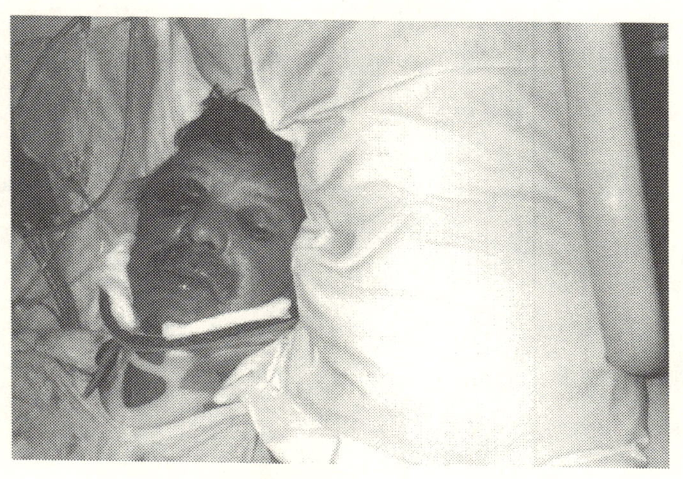

Daddy, bruised and battered, December 2006

He was in the hospital for weeks. He was getting stronger physically, but he became very confused from the head trauma. He was headed to rehab, thank goodness, because there was no way he could go back to Grandma's in this condition. She couldn't handle it. I was relieved because I was hoping they would keep him long enough that he'd be all fixed when he left. I hoped he wouldn't drink, smoke or do anymore bad things. My hopes were high.

The day he was to be transferred to rehab, I walked into the hospital to find he was being released to go home! I was irate! The nurses tried to calm me and explained Daddy had snapped out of it. His mind was back. I had to see for myself. I walked into the room and like they said, he was back! Unfortunately, he was the same, already talking nonsense. He claimed he was beaten up and robbed on the night of the wreck. Then he said a girl was driving the van, not him, and that she fled the scene of the accident. No evidence ever supported this, and he was charged with a DWI, driving with a revoked license, etc., etc. The saddest part was he couldn't wait to get his hands on a cigarette and a beer.

If misfortune and bad luck followed a person, it loved to follow my daddy. He had such an imagination, and sometimes he could draw me into believing him. I should've known better. He was released home to Grandma Chris's house. He went right back to his old ways. Soon, Grandma Chris would go back to Aunt Brenda's to stay. It was for the best!

Would He Ever Find a Place to Call Home?

After Grandma Chris went to live with Aunt Brenda, Daddy was all alone at Grandma Chris's house. She agreed to let him stay there but the bills were too expensive for him alone. Daddy was still drinking and living on the edge. He couldn't care for himself, much less his mother. His health wasn't the best but he could take care of himself. He decided to move.

I found him an apartment in town, just down from his doctor's office. It was across the street from a grocery store and in a safe area. He didn't have a vehicle at this point, so he needed to be in walking distance of as much as possible. My Aunt Brenda and Grandma Chris were gracious enough to let him take some furniture. Erin, our spouses, my mama and I helped him move. I hoped this would be a new start. I had to pay the deposit for the apartment, get the lights turned on and set up the phone, but I didn't mind. Daddy had horrible credit and even though everything was in his name, I had to cosign.

The apartment was a small, one bedroom apartment, not the nicest in the world, but clean. I visited Daddy often at first. I washed dishes and made sure things were clean. He had a bad habit of letting things get dirty, especially himself. That always baffled me. He was always so clean, so well kept. Sometimes, he didn't bathe for days. Did that mean he was falling deeper and deeper into the disease…the alcoholism and the depression?

Just after getting into the apartment, Grandma Chris's home was sold. Daddy got half of the money from it, which was roughly $24,000. Grandma Chris got the other half and since she was living with Aunt Brenda, Aunt Brenda had control over that money. My daddy hated that. He wanted ALL of the money. He really treated my Aunt Brenda very ugly because of that. The love of money is the root of all evil, you know. Once Daddy got his money, he wanted me to put it in my savings account to manage for him. This was the worst mistake of my life! In less than six months, he had blown through roughly $9,000 and I don't know where it went. He would call and need me to transfer money into his account, usually in $500 increments. If I ever questioned him and said no, he'd curse at me and threaten to call the police if I didn't give him his money. Sometimes he would lie and say it was for bills. He was spending his disability check in a week and then dipping into the money I had. He was giving neighbors his Visa debit card, with his PIN, to go to the ATM for him, just a block away! I found out later he was doing drugs of some sort. I was his financial power of attorney, so I had access to his account. I could see all of his transactions and it was unbelievable what was taking place.

Within one year, he was kicked out due to disturbing the neighbors and the landlord didn't want to return the deposit because of how dirty things were. I had to fight to get that deposit back, and thankfully I did.

On to the next apartment search! This apartment was on the other side of town from the one he had. A convenience store was close and that was about it. This apartment was nicer. Everything was clean and new. I cosigned again, and unfortunately had to tell a white lie by omitting the fact that he had just been kicked out of an apartment. I lectured him like a child – no bothering the neighbors, no leaving cigarette butts outside the apartment, keep the apartment clean – this is the LAST time I am moving you! I sounded like a parent talking to his child. My family once again moved him. My mama and the spouses were not as willing this time. He promised he would behave.

Daddy still had money from Grandma Chris's house and he sold his camper. So, he wanted to buy a car since he wasn't now in walking distance of anything. He called me one day and had the Kia salesman at his house with all the paperwork signed to buy a $14,000 brand new Kia Rio. I asked him if he had lost his mind and pleaded with him to get a used car, something cheaper. He didn't want to hear it and said, "I am grown, and I will do what I want." I reminded him this would deplete his money supply. It didn't matter. His mind was made up. He bought the car.

In less than one year, he was kicked out of this apartment for burning a very large hole in the floor. He passed out drunk one night and dropped his cigarette in the floor. Not only did we not get the deposit back, but I had to pay $200 more to cover the cost of the carpet. I was livid! I told him I was done and that he was on his own with moving this time. To my surprise, he found a trailer in a trailer park next to this apartment complex and got all of his things moved. With all of his money gone, again I paid another deposit and cosigned for this trailer that he was renting. Edgewood Mobile Home Park was his final destination. Thankfully, the landlord was very forgiving and overlooked a great deal. This would be where he lived until he left this world.

What had happened? Daddy's dreams of getting a nice trailer on a private lot and dentures so he could smile again were gone. I guess he did have a place to stay and a monthly check and of course, a $14,000 new car. What a waste! Somehow I felt responsible for not saying "No" when he asked for money, but it was his. I felt like he was my child. I longed so much for a father I could lean on, not the other way around.

The Domino Effect

Life for Daddy was worse than ever. Daddy's health was worsening and he was more self-destructive. He had always made bad decisions that put him in awful predicaments, but this was now an understatement.

I once read, "Sin will take you further than you want to go, keep you longer than you want to stay and cost you more than you want to pay." I would say this quote sums up the last ten years of Daddy's life, but it actually sums up the majority of his life. I guess it was just all catching up with him.

He was inching his way into a dark hole and he didn't want to come out. There was a domino effect of misfortune, and I was playing the game. I took on responsibilities I never should have taken. Looking back, I took over where Mama left off years ago. Is there such thing as a "battered daughter syndrome?" If so, I had it. There was also a role reversal. I became the parent and Daddy became the child. We both facilitated it. I enabled him, and he let me! I thought I was helping, but sometimes I was hurting the situation more. I was bitter and mad that my daddy would put me through hardships once again. Sometimes, I wondered why God was punishing me. I became addicted to his drama, even though I wanted no part of it. I needed God to show me the way!

Where do I begin? The new car Daddy purchased wasn't just transportation for him but for everybody else in the neighborhood. The first occurrence went as follows. He called me claiming that somebody had stolen his car. He was yelling at me as if it was my fault. My first question, of course, was "How would someone get the keys to take the car?" Come to find out, a woman he allowed to stay in his house had taken his keys. He didn't even know her last name. He called the police and reported it stolen, but I went on my own criminal investigation. We went to an apartment where he thought she may be, but no one was there. Daddy really wasn't sure if we were even in the right place. Days went by and the police weren't doing anything. I was riding around, checking parking lots for this little burgundy Kia Rio. It was like looking for a needle in a haystack. Crazy enough, in less than a week, I found it. I was on the way from work to Daddy's house. The car was sitting in a parking lot of a restaurant. I picked him up, and we went back to get it. It was unlocked, with the keys in it. I just shook my head in disbelief at how he let a total stranger into his home. I told him so. He always insisted it was someone else's fault – never his.

My advice always went in one ear and out the other. Just a few months later, I got a similar phone call. This time he actually gave the keys to an old girlfriend to borrow the car for a few hours. A few hours turned into a few days. Who did he call? Me! This woman was on drugs, from what Daddy told me. His so-called friends were always very questionable and had addictions similar to his own. This lady kept the car a few weeks. She wouldn't answer the phone, and we couldn't locate the car. He wouldn't call the police on this one. It wasn't really stolen, as I told him, since he gave her the keys. Finally, the girl's sister called Daddy and told him the car was at her parents' home, in their backyard. She had the keys and was willing to give Daddy the car. So, I had to pick Daddy up, go into a dangerous neighborhood, and practically steal the car back while Daddy's ex-girlfriend was asleep. My nerves were all to pieces. I followed Daddy home and walked away shaking my head. Even though I knew my words would be ignored, I still tried to talk to him about making better friends and smarter decisions.

Here is a crazy side story about the ex-girlfriend that kept Daddy's car. They conceived a child together, so Daddy claims. If he was telling the truth, I have a half- sister who is approximately sixteen years old. I guess that's why he wouldn't call the police. Could this be true? I didn't believe it. I didn't let my mind go there.

The next episode came a few months later. This time wasn't as easy as the former. Daddy let a neighbor's wife borrow his car to go to the store, so he thought. She was a drug addict and wasn't actually going to the store, but to buy drugs at a drug house near downtown Greenville. She came back home but not with the car! Daddy called me for help. Daddy went to the husband and asked where the car was and all he got was, "She lost the keys and left it stranded. You shouldn't have let her borrow it." He did get a street address. The street was in an unsafe area beside a drug house. Initially, I didn't go. I didn't know exactly the location. One day, I saw the street and turned down it to see if I could see the car. There it was! No one was around, and I checked to see if it was unlocked. It was. The ignition was torn out. There were dents above the driver's door where someone had broken into the car. No keys were anywhere to be found. It was trashed.

I was so upset and exhausted from the last few months. I had the car towed to Daddy's house and told him I was done, again! He could take it from here. Well it sat in his yard for months. It was apparent he wasn't going to do anything to fix it. He was calling me every day for food and for a ride to the store. I couldn't take it anymore so I asked my brother-in-law, Jimmy, to take a look at it. I wanted to pay to get it fixed, and then I was going to sell it. Daddy agreed. I had the car towed, once again, to Jimmy and Erin's house. The battery was dead so we bought a new battery. Jimmy found a used steering column with the ignition. He put it in and all was fixed.

I bought "For Sale" signs and I put the car on Craigslist. Nothing! So I parked the car at my mama's house. It was a high traffic area and it would get lots of exposure. I had a buyer in less than a week! I had done the research on what the car was worth and I was asking for $7500, not less than $7000. Daddy didn't agree. He wanted more for it, but the car was scratched, dented and had cigarette burns everywhere. Since I was Daddy's power of attorney, I was trumping him on this. I headed to the DMV with the buyers to sign the car over to the new owners. Daddy had given me the paperwork on the car, including the title. The buyers had the check in hand. Then to my horrific surprise, the DMV lady told me I didn't have the title. What I had looked like a title, but it wasn't. Daddy had never gotten one. How could this be? After a great deal of headache and over $500, we had a title. It took several weeks, and Daddy was not very patient.

Finally, the car was sold for $7,000. I called Daddy with the good news. All he wanted was the money. He was mad that I didn't get more for it. During the two weeks it took to get the title, my daddy called me every day, cursing at me. He left messages calling me names and threatening to call the police if I didn't give him his money. I explained that I didn't have it yet. He wasn't hearing it. I felt so hurt and unappreciated. I had already told him that I was going to use the money to get him a new place to live, some dentures and the rest was going in my savings account. I was NOT going to let him blow this money on the same things he had before. He didn't like my idea so I told him he owed me at least $4500 for all the times I bailed him out of jail, all the times I bought him groceries, paid his rent, light bills, etc., not to mention the money for the title and repairs to the car. He told me, "You ought to be ashamed of yourself." I didn't care because I never wanted to be paid back but I had to use this tactic to explain why I was not giving him the money. Well, in the end, he got no dentures, no new place to live. He spent $1000 in a matter of weeks with nothing to show for it and bought a brand new scooter for $1200 to get back and forth to the store. In two weeks, the scooter was stolen. He was back at square one. I still had the rest of the money in my savings account and that's where it stayed.

This was the story of Daddy's life – crazy situations and unthinkable circumstances. Sometimes it didn't feel real. I just wanted him to be normal, to catch a break, to get ahead in life. This is what every parent wants for their child, but this was a child wanting the best for her parent. "I" couldn't make it happen. "I" couldn't fix him. "I" had given it to God so many times but "I" kept taking it back. All that did was put added stress on me. Once again, I prayed. That is really all we can do. Pray and give it to God!

It Was All Taking a Toll

In between all of this craziness, Daddy had quite a few health issues that required surgery. Daddy had very poor blood circulation. It was partly hereditary, but a lot was self-induced by not eating healthy, drinking alcohol, and smoking cigarettes all of his life. He had smoked as much as two packs a day. In the end, his cigarette smoking was more of an addiction than the alcohol.

In his last ten years, Daddy had several surgeries for his vascular problems. Probably eight years ago, his femoral arteries were clogged and he had surgery to open those arteries. It was a very serious and complicated surgery but he rebounded back very quickly. Unfortunately, he didn't change his lifestyle, so he continued to have problems. In his last three to four years, he had two leg surgeries and an abdominal hernia repair. The last surgery was his leg surgery, about a year or so before he died. His leg was in severe pain and it was due to poor circulation. The surgeon needed to put a graft in his vein. At this point, Daddy didn't have many veins or arteries that were his. Daddy had sworn off anymore surgeries because he said, "They don't do any good." I guess this pain was severe enough that he wanted the surgery.

Every time he went through this process, he had to get cardiology clearance because his blood pressure was always elevated. He had medicine but he just wouldn't take it. This particular surgeon had dealt with Daddy so much, he actually didn't make me take him to the cardiologist for this last surgery. Of course, he had to get his pre-op blood work done, chest X-rays, etc. So that was done. Then, anytime he had surgeries or procedures, he couldn't eat or drink after midnight, so I really had to drill that into his head. Usually he always drank a beer the morning of the surgery. He never listened.

I picked him up at 7:30 a.m. to take him to the hospital. He hadn't drunk one beer but numerous beers! He was wasted and in the morning at that! I was so angry, and when I asked him, "What were you thinking?" he responded by cursing and yelling. I didn't say another word. I dropped him off, gave my number to the front desk and left for work. His surgery was to take place around noon, so I figured he'd be sober by then. At 11:00 a.m., I received a phone call that the surgery had been cancelled because his blood alcohol level was too high. Anesthesia wouldn't touch him. I picked him up at the door. I was too embarrassed to go in. He would eventually have the surgery months later with the whole process repeated. Fortunately, he didn't get drunk this time, and the surgery was successful.

Look at all "we" went through to get this done. I wanted to be there for my daddy. I wanted him to have better circulation and be in better health. I think I cared more than him, though. I didn't feel like he appreciated any of what I did to help get him to his appointments. I was breaking my neck to help him, and how did he repay me? He got drunk the morning of surgery. This was why I could get so angry and hurt, not wanting to help him at all. I remember telling him, "This is it. I am done." Then I turned around the next week and took him groceries or made a doctor's appointment for him again. By the way, he never went to his follow-up appointments after surgery. He had his pain medicines, and that's all he wanted anyway.

After countless wrecks, a stroke, a heart attack, roughly five surgeries, years of drinking, drugs and smoking, Daddy was still kicking. I always said he was too mean to die. You just couldn't kill him no matter what. Erin always said he was a cat in his other life because he seemed to have nine lives.

His Cry for Help, Our Last Attempts

Through the years, Daddy had cried wolf a great deal. As you remember when I was younger, he contemplated suicide, never carrying it out. Threatening suicide became more frequent during this time of his life.

He always called drunk. He'd call late at night when I was asleep. I can hear his voice now, slurred and low. "Tracy, I've got a gun in my hand and I'm going to blow my brains out." He'd proceed to talk about the past, and Mama was usually part of the conversation. He might mention family members who had passed away. It would always be sad memories. Most of these conversations ended with him yelling and screaming obscenities. Years ago, I would stay on the phone and talk to him, try to talk him down. I'd get upset. For a moment, I believed he might do it, as I did when I was young. Later in life, I wasn't so compassionate. I didn't fall for it. I couldn't deal with the emotional roller coaster. It's sad to say but on one occasion, I just said, "Fine, do what you have to do." Thank God, he didn't. I couldn't have lived with myself. I know he was crying out for help but I didn't know how to help him. I prayed. Erin and I tried to talk to him. Even my mama pleaded with him to get his life together and have a relationship with his children.

Through the years, Erin tried to reach out to him numerous times, especially after she had children. She wanted them to know their granddaddy. She went to his house several times with her two sons, begging for change. She made a few last attempts the year before he died. Erin and the boys visited him, asking, "Don't you want a relationship with your grandchildren?" His response was, "That's not my bag." He just had his own life, pretty much making it day to day, drinking and smoking. I think a lot of other extracurricular activities I don't know about were involved. There were rumors of continued drug use and prostitutes. Who knows? All we could see was that we were trying to help him, and he was turning us away.

Erin and I had even taken Daddy to church several times, but it never seemed to stick. He always went to the altar to pray too. He cried and played the part, but then it was back to sinful living. There were other sporadic moments when Daddy called me, excited, telling me of how he called the 700 Club. They had prayed with him, and he was inspired. I encouraged him and told him how great that was. I was so hopeful, but unfortunately, it was short-lived.

Aside from the night Daddy died, the last serious talk I had with him about God was about six months before. I said, "Daddy, don't you want to be different? I will help you. I will get you a better place to live and get you cleaned up so your family can come visit you and vice versa." You see, the state would have probably made my daddy move out if they could have seen his house. It was an old trailer, livable, but since Daddy had moved in, he had wrecked the place. It was roach- infested. I had it sprayed more than three times by a professional company. Empty beer cans lined the floor. Cans were in the yard and on the porch. The porch had a horrible stench of urine. Daddy urinated in the empty beer cans instead of going to the bathroom. He slept on the couch and kept blankets hanging up to cover the walkway to the hall and the kitchen. This was to keep the roaches out. The carpet on the floor where his feet rested most of the time was worn down to the wood. It reeked of smoke. Pizza was his food of choice. It was commonplace for at least fifteen to twenty old pizza boxes to be stacked in the corner of the living room. After one of his surgeries a couple of years ago, my husband and his friend went over to Daddy's to clean it so he could come home to a semi-clean house. My husband's friend had to step out and vomit while they were cleaning. They wore masks over their faces and shoe covers. They threw their clothes away when they were done. Side note – every time Daddy had a hospital stay, he was robbed. They'd take the television every time. It was someone he knew. I know it. My husband had to take his television to a friend's nearby whenever he was gone. Crazy stuff!

Wouldn't you want to get out of a house like that? I offered to move him. I asked him again, "Don't you want a relationship with your family?" I tried to paint the perfect picture of a future for him. The answer was always no. I always reiterated, “So you like being miserable, not seeing your family, just making it day to day?” He answered, “Yep.” I’d leave, shaking my head and knowing I had tried.

My Testimony

The last year of Daddy's life, God really worked on me. He showed me things, and my walk with him became closer than it ever had. This closeness to God allowed me to look past Daddy's weaknesses…to forgive him almost daily.

I forgave my daddy many years ago for my childhood. I just never knew things would be the way they were once I grew up and got older. I didn't know Daddy's addiction would continue to affect me, but it did. I had now gone through years of situations with Daddy that had put my emotions to the test. I was trying so hard to do the right thing and honor my father, but was I failing? That is when God revealed something to me.

In early 2013, I was serving on the praise and worship team at University Church of God. My praise and worship pastor, Ernest Silver, had implemented us giving our testimony on any given Sunday prior to service. This was in hopes of strengthening our relationship with the congregation, in turn, having a stronger impact on their salvation. We wanted them to relate to us and get to know us better. I did not volunteer, but was chosen. I had no idea what I was going to talk about. The day I was saved didn't have a big tragedy linked to it. I hadn't hit rock bottom. It definitely was the greatest day of my life but I didn't have a story to embellish it.

I listened each Sunday to the testimonies and talked with Ernest about my concerns. It was then I realized that a testimony didn't have to be about your salvation but how God had worked in your life. So, I thought and thought. Aha, I had it! Not until I was asked to share my testimony did I even know I had one. Thank you Ernest! I was astonished at what the Lord gave me. My testimony was two-part – two situations in my life that collided and not until now did I even put the two together. It is amazing how God intervenes on our behalf and we have no knowledge of it until it helps us the most.

After Dexter and I married in April 2003, I wanted to start trying to get pregnant. I was on birth control pills but was still hesitant to stop. Of course, I thought I would get pregnant quickly. I was thirty-one when I got married. Two years later, I stopped taking my pills. I really wanted a baby. Dexter was fine either way. We had a beautiful son, DJ, my stepson, but I wanted a girl. Call me selfish. I haven't talked a great deal about myself but I'm a solution-oriented person. I'm a fix-it kind of person. I'm also a nurse, so no matter what the problem, I'm going to make it right, fix it or find someone who can. In the last few years of my daddy's life and in the midst of trying to get pregnant, I learned I didn't have to do it all alone. God is and was there all along.

After I stopped taking birth control pills, a year went by and I didn't get pregnant. I didn't panic at first, but after another year, my emotions got the best of me. I set up appointments at the fertility doctor and had Dexter checked out – I wish you could've seen his face. The doctors couldn't find anything wrong. I was willing to go only so far with fertility. I was willing to take medication for ovulation and even intra-uterine insemination, but that would be the extent. The roller coaster ride began. I tried to de-stress my life. That was a joke! I even changed jobs in 2006, hoping to decrease my stress. "I" was going to make it happen. Guess what, it didn't. Every month was the same. My cycle was late, and I got excited. Then my cycle started, so I cried and felt sorry for myself. The next month, it would all start over again. I prayed every day and night God would give me a baby.

One day I was at Mama's house talking about the fertility doctor and what I had been doing to try to get pregnant. My granny, bless her sweet soul, said "You're stepping on God's toes. You'll get pregnant in God's timing." At that point, I realized I had been doing it all wrong. I remember praying and crying to God that night. I just apologized over and over. I told God if he didn't see fit for me to have a child, I was fine with that. I wanted his will to be done, not mine. I stopped everything, the fertility visits, the medications, everything! Well, with the exception of sex, that is. We still had to do that once in a while! Time would pass without a positive pregnancy test, but I was much better with it. I knew God was controlling it and I didn't have to.

Let's move forward to 2009. I still wasn't pregnant. I wasn't stressed any longer about getting pregnant but Daddy's life was still in upheaval. Do you remember all of the DWIs I mentioned previously? Well, they were never resolved. It's like they vanished into thin air until now! In 2008, Pitt County started going back in the archives, pulling those old court cases. Guess who the lucky winner was. You got it, Daddy! Daddy was assigned a state-appointed lawyer because, at this point, his finances were limited and his health wasn't good. He missed court dates and had been picked up twice and taken to jail. I bailed him out both times. A friend of mine was a bail bondsman and only charged me 10%. Between the two times, I spent around $1000. I couldn't keep doing this. I was the one he always called. I felt helpless and all I could do was pray. On February 6, 2009, he got picked up again for not going to court. The bad thing is the lawyer was going to have everything thrown out if he had only gone to court that day. So I received the collect call and didn't answer. I went to Mama's house and told her about it. She told me to leave him in jail, so I called Ernest for some spiritual guidance. I was torn on what to do. I knew I should leave him there but I felt badly leaving him in jail. Ernest told me of a story about his brother, who had similar problems. He talked to me about enabling, and he quoted Scripture to inspire me.

As a Christian, I always struggled with my relationship with Daddy. He could make it so hard but I didn't want to disrespect him. I wanted to do the right thing but sometimes I didn't know what that was. I decided to leave him in jail. I got word to him of my decision and explained that if he stayed in jail for a month, everything would be resolved. What choice did he have? I actually felt at peace with my decision. I knew I was obeying God.

On March 6, 2009, Daddy was released from jail and on March 6, my pregnancy test turned positive. I believe with all my heart that obedience to God regarding my daddy resulted in the blessing of a child. And guess what? It was a girl, Tori, born November 2009. I never worried a day of my pregnancy because I knew it was God's plan, not mine. "In God's timing," – that's what my Granny always said, and she was right!

My beautiful family – Dexter, Tori and me, 2012

Isn't it amazing how my daddy was at the center of it all…my testimony anyway? God was truly at the center of it all, but who would've ever thought that my blessing, Tori, would be a result of my obedience to God with regards to Daddy. It took me until 2013 to have this revelation which, again, was in God's timing. He knew I needed this before the next step.

The End, the Beginning

It's 7:00 p.m. on December 22, 2013. I knew Daddy was on the way to the hospital and he'd be fine just like always. I was going to call the hospital in an hour to check on him. I continued celebrating Christmas with my family. No more than a half hour had gone by, and my phone rang. It was the hospital number, and immediately I felt anxious. I answered, and it was a social worker. She asked if I had plans to come to the hospital because she needed some information on Daddy. He had been there numerous times and twice in the last few months, so I didn't understand what she could possibly need. I told her I was waiting until the doctors had Daddy squared away. Then I had planned to call to check on him. She politely informed me the doctors were already working on him and strongly urged me to come to the hospital. I hung up, looked at my family and told them I was needed at the hospital. I left and headed for the hospital.

On the way to the hospital, I called Dr. Goldstein. He is a wonderful gastroenterologist and even better boss. He completed an upper endoscopy within the past year on my daddy, and I couldn't remember what he found. He recalled there being a small esophageal ulcer and reassured me by explaining the ulcer could be worse, maybe bleeding. That would explain Daddy throwing up blood, and the chunks were probably clots. I was relieved somewhat, but I still couldn't shake this feeling.

When I arrived at the hospital, it was just me. I was escorted to the trauma bay where his weak body lay. He was awake and talking to me. I remember so many nurses and doctors coming in and out. He had on a blood-splattered gown, and I could see where an attempt was made to clean blood off the floor. The nurse confirmed he had just vomited a huge amount of blood, and rescue workers said his living room floor was covered in it. Daddy was as pale as a ghost. His face and neck always looked red because of the alcohol, but today he looked a dusky, pale gray. His blood pressure reading was 80/60, and I immediately told the nurse that if this was accurate, then he was really sick. His blood pressure usually ran 200/110. She replied right away, "Oh yeah, we know. He is really sick." I asked Daddy what he had been eating or drinking, of course, thinking he had caused this somehow. With dried blood in the creases of his mouth, he whispered, "I haven't eaten anything in the last few days, and I haven't drank any alcohol in three days."

I then looked to the nurse to see if a gastroenterologist had been consulted so that I could make sure my doctor was called. They had already notified him, but he wanted lab work on Daddy to ensure stability before doing anything. Dr. Marcuard was on call that night. He is my other boss and an equally wonderful gastroenterologist. I immediately called him and the first thing he asked was, "Is it your daddy?" When I said yes, he replied, "I will be right there." I told the nurses about Daddy's ulcer, and I think we were all hoping that's what it was. Daddy kept saying he could feel more blood coming. I tried to reassure him, "I'm here, and I love you." He asked me not to leave, and I told him I'd be right there.

Erin and Jimmy then arrived. I think Erin was like me. She wasn't planning on coming to the hospital either. Mama said something to her about going, and that's all it took to get her here. They went to his bedside to offer their love and reassurance. We stepped away to let the nurses work. The doctor told us we could stay right outside the curtain of the trauma bay, so we got comfortable on a stretcher just outside his curtain. Erin, the social network butterfly, got busy calling and texting everyone. She reached out to her Facebook family to start praying. I was so glad she was there because my mind was somewhere else, and I couldn't even focus on any of that at the moment. In my mind, I kept praying for God to help me and for His will to be done.

The nurses informed us they were going to start a central line in Daddy's neck and it might be painful for him, so we could go to the family room. The social worker that called earlier came around about that time and needed to get some information from us anyway. We went to Daddy's bedside and explained what they were doing, then told him we'd be right back. He nodded OK. They were giving him blood, and he was somewhat stable at the time.

We gave the social worker what she needed, and I started asking what we could do to get Daddy help once he went home…a nurse's aide to help him bathe, perhaps, and help with daily activities? Unfortunately, he needed Medicaid for that, and he only had Medicare. Years ago, after his Christmas Eve wreck, I tried to get Medicaid for him. He didn't have enough debt and made too much in his disability check. Nothing had changed! The social worker was very nice, but she couldn't give us the answers we needed. She prayed with us, though, and that meant the world to me.

We were called back to Daddy's trauma bay. The nurse informed us he had just vomited another large amount of blood. They had him cleaned up, but he still looked so weak. The doctor told us Daddy would need to be sedated so they could care for him better. We agreed. The doctor then encouraged us to talk to Daddy one last time before he was sedated. My heart sunk. We walked in and told Daddy the doctor was going to sedate him, but we wouldn't leave his side. Again, I told him I loved him and stepped away so Erin could talk to him. When she was done, I let her go in front of me out of the room. I was the last to walk away but before I reached the end of his bed, I felt a tug in my heart that physically turned my body around. I walked up to his ear and whispered, "Daddy, you need to get saved. I know you believe, and I know you want to go to heaven." He nodded yes and I said, "I need to hear you say it!" To my surprise, he whispered "Yes!" I got closer to his face, and we prayed, "God, please forgive him of his sins. He believes in you and wants to go to heaven. In Jesus' name we pray, Amen." He nodded yes with his head the entire time I prayed.

I walked away and went to the stretcher where Erin and Jimmy sat. She started crying. The reality had set in. He might not make it this time. I immediately told her, "It's OK, it's ok, he just got saved!" She was in shock! "What?" they said. I told them how the Lord turned me around and allowed me to try one last time to lead Daddy to Christ. We all cried.

Dr. Marcuard finally arrived and began doing the endoscopy. I watched the whole thing. There was old, dark brown blood all throughout the esophagus and stomach. At the end of the test, there it was – a pulsating bulge squirting blood every time it pulsated! It was a bleeding artery. The hole had tunneled into Daddy's stomach. Not only was he throwing up blood, but it was oozing from his rectum now. My doctor was in amazement. He pulled out the scope and ordered a vascular consult STAT! My doctor reassured me a surgeon would come in and fix everything. He told me it was going to be a long night, so I could take the next day off.

Daddy had an arterial graft in his abdominal aorta. It was placed years ago by a surgeon in town to help with poor blood circulation. The doctors were thinking something may have happened to the graft. They paged the surgeon, and we waited. I had arrived at the hospital around 7:30 p.m., and it was after 10:00 p.m. now. I was anxious but at peace. I didn't know how this night would end. I was so proud of my sister. She was so strong. She doesn't usually do well with "blood and guts," but she was hanging in there.

The surgeon finally arrived. We knew each other very well. I had taken Daddy to his office often and corresponded with him regarding Daddy's health on numerous occasions. He shook his head and told me it wasn't good. Either the aorta was ruptured or the graft was infected and had caused a rupture. With either scenario, Daddy was malnourished and wouldn't survive the surgery. But if we didn't do surgery, Daddy would die! I looked at Erin, and then I looked up to God. In my mind, I said, "I don't know what to do Lord. Help me." I looked straight ahead and the next thing I heard from behind the curtain was "He's coding!" The trauma doctor came to me and said, "We are doing CPR but it's not circulating blood to his brain. We will keep on if you want." I told him to continue for a few more minutes. A few minutes later, he came back and said he was stopping CPR. I agreed. His death was called just after 11:00 p.m. It was done. He was gone. Erin, Jimmy and I cried, but rejoiced. We were in awe...in awe of God's work.

I don't know if you saw all the ways God intervened on this night to help ensure my daddy's salvation, but we did! God put us where we needed to be, when we needed to be there. I cried for sheer gratefulness that God had allowed this. God didn't give up on my daddy! This type of condition usually kills a person in less than thirty minutes. Most people bleed to death in their sleep or before healthcare workers can get to them. Not today! The social worker who got me to the hospital was God's angel. Then God himself met me there at Daddy's bedside. And right when I was faced with the decision about surgery, the Lord took him! What an awesome God!

My mama came to the hospital just after Daddy died. She was so upset. She was always so heartbroken over how Daddy's life had turned out. She loved him. He was the father of her two children. She had to see him one last time. Ernest came to check on us, offering his support. He escorted Mama to see Daddy, along with Jimmy. I didn't want to go with them. I had an image of him I wanted to keep in my mind. Erin stayed with me right outside the door. We were at peace with everything and still engulfed with the awesome events of the night...the work of God. Thank you God for your grace!

I know the night Daddy died, each step was ordered by the Lord. Daddy always called me for all of his problems, but in the end, I think he really tried not to burden me. In October and November of 2013, Daddy was hospitalized twice. One of the times was because he passed out on the couch. There was some lady living with him, and she called 911. Normally he would call me immediately, but this time he only called me to pick him up. I think his blood sugar was low, but they couldn't find anything else wrong. The other time he was having chest pain and called 911 on his own. It was a mild heart attack that time but, again, he only called me to pick him up…not before. I told him he was a ticking time bomb, but he didn't believe me or he just didn't care. The night he died, he called me immediately. I know, without a doubt, if he had waited or gone to the hospital without calling me, I wouldn't have gotten the chance to pray with him!

One of our last pictures taken of Daddy, Christmas of 2009

The Funeral

The next week was a blur. We all tried to get some sleep the night Daddy died, but I don't think we did. I actually went to work the next day. Everyone thought I was crazy, but I had to keep moving. Plus, I was anxious. We had a funeral to plan, and Christmas was in three days.

Erin and I met with the funeral home that Monday, the 23rd, and decided his funeral would be on December 26th. In just a matter of hours, we had the funeral planned. God provided everything we needed. It seemed effortless. Our families, friends, and our church families showed up during this time of need, despite the holidays. Erin's preacher, Pastor Gene Williams of Parker's Chapel Free Will Baptist Church, agreed to conduct the funeral.

All we needed were songs. I immediately knew Ernest Silver had to sing, "Were It Not for Grace." The words of the song described Daddy's situation perfectly, and only Ernest's angelic voice could do it justice. This song describes how if our salvation were left up to us, we'd be lost; we'd be running and losing the race, were it not for grace. Please listen to this song, and let it speak to you.

Daddy grew up listening to country music, but he also loved those traditional hymns we sang at Bell Arthur Christian Church. We agreed to play one of Daddy's favorite hymns. We chose Carrie Underwood's rendition of "How Great Thou Art." What a powerful song!

We wanted one more song, a song to represent Daddy. We needed it to represent his life, his circumstances, his struggles and then his victory. We chose the song, "Changed," sung by Rascal Flatts. They are an amazingly talented group who probably never knew that one day this song would be my Daddy's theme song. In a moment, my daddy was changed…by the grace of God. He would never be the same again. We dedicated this song to Daddy. My favorite part of the song is when they describe how life can get off track. We can make mistakes, backslide and be lost. BUT if we fall down on our knees and give it all to God, we can be CHANGED! Listen to this song in its entirety. It will move you!

Between the awesome word of Pastor Gene and the songs, there wasn't a dry eye in the church. I believe souls were touched that day…even saved!

I wanted to share the sermon that was preached that day for one reason and one reason only – to win souls to Christ. What I will share with you on paper will not come close to reaching the profoundness of the word that day or how Pastor Gene delivered it.

Pastor Gene stood at the front of that church in silence. He looked stern – very serious – almost at a loss for words. He began explaining how he came to know my daddy, which was through Erin. He knew of Daddy's struggles and addictions. He knew how it had affected Erin. He shared that with everyone. He didn't hold back. He actually stated, "I'm not going to sugar-coat this." He painted the picture accurately of Daddy, running from the Lord and chasing sin. It was pretty harsh, but true. There was a point when I thought to myself, where is he going with this? But as soon as I did, he brought it home to Scripture. He began to correlate Daddy's life with the thief on the cross. This is the thief who committed sin his entire life, the thief who mocked Jesus on the cross, but also the thief who chose to believe and give his heart to Jesus just before his death. Luke 23:32-43. He went on to say that in Daddy's final hour, like the thief who repented, Daddy also received the Lord. "This last minute path is not the best way, the preferred way, or sometimes even a way at all for some people, but thanks to God, it was the way for Van that night." Then, he looked dead into the hearts of everyone there, and asked, "Are some of you angry about that? Do some of you think that's not fair, that someone can sin their entire life and in their last moments here get to right it all? Well, that's the God we serve. You can be saved at a young age or on your death bed, and God will accept you either way if you sincerely choose to give yourself to him and believe." His words were piercing and even though there was no altar call, I believe someone gave his heart to the Lord that day.

He ended his sermon by reading something I wrote for Daddy and for everyone in attendance that day.

The Eulogy

Most of you remember Daddy when he was a vibrant, handsome, fun-loving guy with a smile that lit up the room. Like us all, he has had his struggles and fought many demons. For ALL of his family – sister, brothers, daughters and grandchildren – he loved us all in his own way. Daddy skirted death more times than I can remember, and God spared his life every time. I thank God for directing every step on December 22, 2013. Daddy had a condition that would usually take a life instantly, but God gave us grace by giving my sister and me time to get to the hospital to say our goodbyes. During those last moments, we were given the honor of seeing our daddy repent and give his heart to God. I prayed for Daddy's salvation many a night, wondering if God had knocked for the last time and closed the door forever. I realized on the night Daddy died that God loves us all in our good and bad. All God wants is for us to come to him. He loves us all the same, whether we do it as a youngster in church or as a sixty-five year old man on his death bed. My daddy experienced a "change" just before he died. Not all of us will be that fortunate. My sister and I are playing the song "Changed" as a tribute to Daddy and hope it will inspire anyone who is not saved to give their life to God sooner rather than later.

After the song ended, we stood in a line – greeting everyone – hugging and crying. I had family members tell me it was the best funeral they had ever attended. I felt proud. I felt a sense of accomplishment because I knew Daddy was looking down from heaven, a place I never thought he would go. Over sixty people came out that day even with the holidays upon us. The kind words sent from family and friends via texts and Facebook were overwhelming. We felt extremely loved.

After eating a hearty meal provided by the church, my family headed to the graveside. Daddy had requested numerous times in the past to be cremated. Of course, his vision of the funeral was down at Seine Beach in Grimesland. This is where we went boat riding every summer for years when I was young. He wanted family and friends to be present as we spread his ashes in the river. In between those requests, he'd change his mind and say, "You might as well bury me in the Nichols cemetery in Bell Arthur." We would give him the best of both worlds. We'd bury half of his ashes in the Nichols Cemetery and spread the other half in the river at Seine Beach.

At the graveside, my closest family members and friends were gathered. My immediate family was present including my husband, daughter, Mama, her husband and Erin's family. Daddy's siblings, Aunt Brenda and Uncle Wayne were right there. Aunt Teresa, my late Uncle Jerry's wife, came also. All my cousins were in attendance with their families. Mama and Daddy's closest friends throughout their marriage were there, Johnny and Gloria. They were right by Mama's side. Daddy lost touch or alienated many of the ones in attendance, but they still showed up in a powerful way. It was moving!

The preacher didn't come to the graveside, so I stood up and thanked everyone for coming. I knew Daddy's relationship had been strained with his siblings, so I tried to reassure them. "He loved us all the best way he knew how. He gave all he could." We rejoiced in the fact he was in heaven now. God took him at just the right time…a time that guaranteed his salvation. We all shared a memory of Daddy. We laughed and cried. Then Aunt Teresa mentioned how Daddy always loved the song, "Amazing Grace." Her granddaughter, Shelby, led us in a verse. It was a great family moment.

My brother in law, Jimmy, dug the hole where my Daddy's ashes would reside. He took great pride in doing so. I felt so very blessed. My family had really come together to honor Daddy's memory. I will never forget this day!

Inspired Words – The Great Reversal Sermon

My pastor, Wayne Flora, attended Daddy's funeral. He was inspired by the words Pastor Gene spoke that day. Pastor Wayne called me a week after the funeral to ask if he could include Daddy and his story in his sermon on January 4. I was honored, and responded, "Of course."

After Daddy died, Pastor Wayne called me to offer his condolences. It was then I told him about God's grace and how the Holy Spirit moved the night Daddy died. I shared with him the words I spoke to Daddy. I shared this with him on December 23rd and never spoke of it again. On January 4th, he quoted me almost word for word in his sermon. Amazing!

I want to share his sermon with you as well because there are people who need it. It is inspiring and motivating. It will give hope to the hopeless. It will show you, as it did me, no matter how deep in sin we may be or how lost we are, it is never too late!

THE GREAT REVERSAL! (Or LET'S BE SURE!)

(The Actual Sermon)

Mt. 20:1-16

Jan. 4, 2014

By Pastor Wayne Flora

MSG

20 [1-2] "God's kingdom is like an estate manager who went out early in the morning to hire workers for his vineyard. They agreed on a wage of a dollar a day, and went to work.

[3-5] "Later, about nine o'clock, the manager saw some other men hanging around the town square unemployed. He told them to go to work in his vineyard and he would pay them a fair wage. They went.

[5-6] "He did the same thing at noon, and again at three o'clock. At five o'clock he went back and found still others standing around. He said, 'Why are you standing around all day doing nothing?'

[7] "They said, 'Because no one hired us.'

"He told them to go to work in his vineyard.

[8] "When the day's work was over, the owner of the vineyard instructed his foreman, 'Call the workers in and pay them their wages. Start with the last hired and go on to the first.'

[9-12] "Those hired at five o'clock came up and were each given a dollar. When those who were hired first saw that, they assumed they would get far more. But they got the same, each of them one dollar. Taking the dollar, they groused angrily to the manager, 'These last workers put in only one easy hour, and you just made them equal to us, who slaved all day under a scorching sun.'

[13-15] "He replied to the one speaking for the rest, 'Friend, I haven't been unfair. We agreed on the wage of a dollar, didn't we? So take it and go. I decided to give to the one who came last the same as you. Can't I do what I want with my own money? Are you going to get stingy because I am generous?'

[16] "Here it is again, the Great Reversal: many of the first ending up last, and the last first."

KJV

2Pe 1:10 Wherefore the rather, brethren, give diligence to make your calling and election sure: for if ye do these things, ye shall never fall:

MSG

[10-11] So, friends, confirm God's invitation to you, his choice of you. Don't put it off; do it now. Do this, and you'll have your life on a firm footing, the streets paved and the way wide open into the eternal kingdom of our Master and Savior, Jesus Christ.

Introduction

On Dec. 22, just prior our celebration of Christmas, Robert "Van" Nichols, age 65, was seriously stricken in his health and was rushed to the hospital for emergency treatment. It was determined that he was suffering an internal bleeding crisis, and while momentarily intercepted, the family was faced with a critical decision about life support – the odds were not in his favor.

His daughter, our own Tracy Morrisey, herself a medical professional, was not unrealistic about his situation. She knew that her father, for whom she has prayed for years and years for his spiritual need, had once walked with Christ, but that many years of spiritual waywardness and carnal strongholds had taken its toll upon his body…and his soul, and that at this critical moment in his life, he was *not likely ready to meet God.*

The medical team in place, as she walked away from his bedside, the Holy Spirit instructed her to go back to him – no matter who was temporarily put off by this succinct and decisive obedience – to challenge her dad to accept Christ and make his choice for Jesus before he might draw his last breath!

"Dad, you KNOW you believe in God!" "Yes," he responds. "You know you believe Jesus is God's Son!" "Yes," he says. "You know you must believe in him and accept him as your personal Savior to have eternal life and to go to heaven!" "Yes," he replies. "Dad, I need to hear you say it – I need to know you truly trust Jesus for your salvation – I need to know you are going to heaven! Do you understand what I'm saying?" ***And right there, Tracy led her father into a real and personal, intimate relationship with Jesus Christ!***

Right upon the heels of that eternally-breath-taking moment, when she was *pressed to make a decision* about life support – *he coded.* And left this world a born-again child of God, a member of the family of the redeemed, and instantly awakened in the arms of Jesus the split second he transitioned!

> **WAIT A MINUTE! THAT'S NOT FAIR! I'VE SERVED GOD ALL MY LIFE AND LABORED EXHAUSTIVELY IN THE CHURCH AND CHRISTIAN SERVICE! I'VE TAUGHT SUNDAY SCHOOL, SANG IN THE CHOIR, KEPT THE NURSERY, SERVED ON CHURCH BOARDS – AND PAID MY TITHE – MY FAITHFUL 10% OF ALL MY INCOME ALL MY LIFE – *AND YOU'RE TELLING ME HE GETS THE SAME GIFT OF ETERNAL LIFE I GET? AND ALL HE DID WAS PRAYED A SIMPLE, 30-SECOND PRAYER?!***

That's right! That's exactly what I'm saying!

I was in awe when I heard Tracy's story. My wife and I attended his funeral the following Thursday, the day after Christmas.

Pastor Gene Williams of the Parkers Free Will Baptist Church officiated. He knew this family well.

I was amazed by his message – so profoundly – that I went right to him after the service and told him how deeply I honored and respected him – for not only being personal and compassionate with this grieving family, but also being truthful – speaking God's Word so plainly, NO ONE could have misunderstood. There were unbelievers there that day that needed to hear those words.

I have never heard anyone define *"death-bed repentance,"* but Pastor Williams did. He clearly explained that a death bed repentance is one that when a person repents of his sin and trusts Jesus for his salvation that ***"if it were possible in that very moment in his life to go back and undo EVERYTHING he had ever done wrong, he would do it!"*** Then Jesus, seeing *and knowing* his heart ACCEPTS HIS REPENTANCE and treats him just as if HE HAD NEVER COMMITTED the first sin!

WOW! What a description of authentic, biblical repentance! BUT AFTER ALL, ISN'T THAT WHAT REAL REPENTANCE FOR ANY OF US IS?!

Thief on the Cross

"Hey," you say, *"Isn't that what happened to the thief on the cross?"*

Yeah, but not right away! Matthew sets the stage for the early hours on the cross, and Luke tells us the end result.

GW

Mat 27:38 At that time they crucified two criminals with him, one on his right and the other on his left.

Mat 27:39 Those who passed by insulted him. They shook their heads

Mat 27:40 and said, "You were going to tear down God's temple and build it again in three days. Save yourself! If you're the Son of God, come down from the cross."

Mat 27:41 The chief priests together with the scribes and the leaders made fun of him in the same way. They said,

Mat 27:42 "He saved others, but he can't save himself. So he's Israel's king! Let him come down from the cross now, and we'll believe him.

Mat 27:43 He trusted God. Let God rescue him now if he wants. After all, this man said, 'I am the Son of God.'"

Mat 27:44 Even the criminals crucified with him were insulting him the same way.

- Is death-bed repentance possible? You'd better believe it! Is God love? Is truth righteous? Is Jesus the Son of God?

In the short time between when these thieves were placed on their crosses on either side of Jesus Christ, God's Son, 'till when they died – *Yes, for crimes they committed! For debts to society they owed!* – SOMETHING HAPPENED! SOMETHING GLORIOUS HAPPENED!

One of them witnessed the revelation of Jesus' being God's Son – SOMETHING changed his mind! He opened his heart to the truth of Gospel message!

1. **First, he MOCKED!**

2. **Then, he MEDITATED!**

3. **Finally, he MADE A DECISION! To trust Jesus in his dying breath!**

KJV

Luk 23:39 And one of the malefactors which were hanged railed on him, saying, If thou be Christ, save thyself and us.

Luk 23:40 But the other answering rebuked him, saying, Dost not thou fear God, seeing thou art in the same condemnation?

Luk 23:41 And we indeed justly; for we receive the due reward of our deeds: but this man hath done nothing amiss.

Luk 23:42 And he said unto Jesus, Lord, remember me when thou comest into thy kingdom.

Luk 23:43 And Jesus said unto him, Verily I say unto thee, To day shalt thou be with me in paradise.

FAST LESSONS FROM THIS SCENE

1. ***ANYONE can be saved if he will ONLY believe in and accept Jesus as the Son of God!*** **This penitent thief dying on a cross didn't have any time whatsoever to get down off the cross, go make recompense for all his ill deeds, come back and make an offering to God for all his sin!**
2. ***ANYBODY can watch ANYONE ELSE get saved only 15 feet away – watch and hear him accept Jesus, repent of his sins, receive eternal life – AND YET HE HIMSELF STILL DIE IN HIS SINS AND SPEND ETERNITY IN HELL!*** **That you come from a Christian family, even attend church – DOESN'T MAKE YOU A CHRISTIAN! You can be around it all your life, then stand before God and say so – but if you haven't personally repented of your sins and trusted**

Jesus for your salvation, YOU ARE NOT READY FOR HEAVEN!

Transition: What other important *lessons* do we learn from this analogy of the landowner-estate manager that prompts us to be ready for heaven?

REVIEW THE MT. 20 STORY

A. Getting saved has NOTHING to do with good works, but EVERYTHING to do with God's grace!

KJV

- **Isaiah 64:6** But we are all as an unclean *thing, and all our righteousnesses are as filthy rags;* and we all do fade as a leaf; and our iniquities, like the wind, have taken us away [from God].
- You and I have NOTHING to bring to God that could persuade him we deserve heaven! Nothing!
- Not accomplishments, achievements, great feats of inspiration, education, degrees, ambitions, skills, sacrifices, fiscal wizardry, great wealth, popularity, prestige, reputation, glamour, or good looks! **NONE OF THESE COUNT FOR ANYTHING IN THE KINGDOM –** ***BUT a humble heart and contrite spirit, a broken vessel and sincere faith – THAT'S WHAT TOUCHES THE HEART OF GOD!***

B. Getting saved has NOTHING to do with <u>fairness</u>, but EVERYTHING to do with <u>faithfulness</u>!

- GOD'S FAITHFULNESS – not yours! Not mine! His faithfulness to himself and his own goodness and His promises to have relationship with anyone who trusts Jesus for salvation!
- Terribly misconceived in this text to imagine that God rewards us SALVATION based upon how hard we work! Truth is, He's ***"OVER-REWARDING"*** those who worked the least! Notice:
    - **KJV** - *"agreed with the laborers"* amount of pay – considered "fair" by both parties
    - **CEV** - *"the usual amount for a day's work"* – at the end of the day when the foreman distributes pay, NO ONE IS BEING CHEATED – the landowner is paying everyone what each agreed; but in fact, he is choosing of his own accord to be as generous to those who worked a little as those who worked a lot!
    - **...and says, *"Can't I do what I want with my own money? Are you going to be jealous (stingy) because I so generous to others besides you?***
- **WHAT'S THE LESSON HERE? The lesson is NONE of us deserved to be saved! None of us earned salvation! None of us had a hope in heaven of ever going IF GOD HAD NOT BEEN <u>MERCIFUL TO US ALL</u>!**

- ***Whether <u>FIRST IN</u> or <u>LAST IN</u> is no matter! WHAT MATTERS IS THAT WE MAKE IT IN!***
- If you really want what's "fair," then "what's fair" is that you and I should miss heaven, end up in hell, and never have a hope of the love of God ever again – never have a hope of everlasting life! THAT'S FAIR!
- **God doesn't save us because it's "fair" – He saves us because he's merciful, and loves us, and gladly pays the price for our salvation in His own Son's death on the cross! THERE'S NOTHING FAIR ABOUT THAT!**

C. Getting saved has NOTHING to do with <u>volume</u>, but EVERYTHING to do with <u>content</u>!

- How <u>long</u> you've served Christ is meaningful, but not nearly as important as <u>how diligently</u>!
- There are young Christians who are <u>spiritually mature</u> – and there are aged Christians who are still <u>spiritual babes</u>.
- The writer of Hebrews acknowledges to his readers in 5:12, **BBE** - *"And though by this time it would be right for you to be teachers, you still have need of someone to give you teaching about the first simple rules of God's revelation; you have become like babies who have need of milk, and not of solid food."*
- **The length of life is not nearly as critical as the quality of it!** I'll never forget the sadness I felt after a couple of hours on Mackinaw Island, Michigan in a butterfly sanctuary where hundreds and hundreds of exotic butterflies would

perch like pets on my arms and shoulders and head. Greatest joy of entire trip! Then I learned as I left that the average lifespan of an adult butterfly was 10 days to 2 weeks. I'll always remember what the attendant at the door said when I mentioned how sad I thought that was – ***"Oh, but that butterfly with its hundreds of eyes will enjoy more of life in 10 days than most people will in 80 years!"***

CONCLUSION:

God doesn't judge as we; His standards are higher than ours! We judge the work of man's hands – God the work of his heart!

I'm hearing God say, "Get them ready!" There must be a reason – why I shared with you THE GREAT REVERSAL, which the subtitle could easily be "LET'S ALL BE SURE!"

I would like to think EVERYONE in this house has eternal life, ready for heaven, prepared to meet God...odds are, that's not so!

Van Nichols' story is a moving example of how generous and gracious our loving God is – but not everyone can hope for those final few breaths and conscious capacity to make that all-important decision to accept Christ right before "lights out..."

- Some of us here will die suddenly, no warning...
- Heart attack, stroke, blood clot, aneurysm...
- Automobile accident, house fire...maybe murder – I pray not!

- BUT STATISTICAL ODDS SAY SO!
- When that happens, death-bed repentance isn't an option! The accountability EACH OF US HAS for knowing Christ is ANSWERED…
- RIGHT NOW! IN THIS MOMENT!
- IN THIS SERVICE! DURING THIS PRAYER!
- II Cor. 6:2 "Now accepted time – today day of salvation!"

MSG

[10-11] So, friends, confirm God's invitation to you, his choice of you. Don't put it off; do it now! Do this, and you'll have your life on a firm footing, the streets paved and the way wide open into the eternal kingdom of our Master and Savior, Jesus Christ!

*The night he left this world, I knew I would finally have the daddy I always wanted and needed...**It would just be in heaven!***

God's Not Done Yet!

What an amazing journey! So many struggles, so much pain, but then the miraculous power of the Lord prevailed. Daddy was in heaven. It was done…over. But was it? When the Lord first placed this book in my spirit, I thought he just wanted me to share the stories – the stories of the past and Daddy's last night here. However, as I started writing, God placed urgency in my heart – an urgency to get his word out to whoever needed it. I would lay down at night to pray with such a heavy heart of guilt – guilt for not writing daily. I prayed for guidance. I prayed for time to write. I wanted to obey God and most importantly, I wanted his will to be done.

So, God answered my prayers. Ernest called me one morning, knowing my struggles with not being able to write as much as I wanted, and he shared with me how God had placed something in his spirit that he felt led to share with me. He gave me encouragement by confirming the urgency was a good thing. It reinforced that this story was really meant to touch the lives of many. He recommended I start a blog or an internet page with insights into the book, inspirational words that could reach people now! At the time, I didn't know what I'd write, so I prayed.

My closest friend and co-worker, Jazett, and probably my biggest cheerleader with regards to the book, developed a Facebook page. We titled it *Just in Time*, of course, and placed a beautiful picture in the background with the Scripture that describes it all, 2 Corinthians 12:9, "My grace is sufficient for you, for my power is made perfect in weakness." We sent invitations to over one hundred fifty friends, explaining the book and asking for prayers during the writing process, while also encouraging everyone to share the upcoming insights with all of their friends.

Every day, I prayed for a word from the Lord, and he answered. Sometimes, it was once a week and sometimes every two weeks. I tried more than ever to really listen to God for his instruction. It was amazing what he gave to me. God showed me that all of the past – and even that last night – was important, but the life lessons learned from those experiences was what God wanted to show you and me!

As God gave me the words to share with everyone, I learned so much about myself. I came to terms with things I did so wrong and realized I could do things differently in the future. He showed me there were others in the world going through the same situations I went through in the past. He revealed friends of mine who were still holding on to hurt, disappointment, and bitterness. God showed me there was more to be done! My daddy's journey was over, but there were others whose journeys had just begun.

I hope and pray these life lessons – "Guidelines from God" – speak to you the way they spoke to me. I may have written the words, but God is the true author!

July 30, 2014 – **The Addiction Took My Daddy from Me**

The writing process was slow. I had written about numerous memories from the past, but there was no order to anything I had written. I felt inadequate, and I doubted myself. That is when the Lord began to help me. He began flooding my mind with what he wanted in the book, while also giving me the life lessons. These life lessons would encourage me while writing, but would also be guidelines for you and me to live by. This first entry sums up everything – the struggle and the victory. Most importantly, it reaffirms how we need God in our lives. We need him to guide us and protect us – sometimes even from ourselves.

For so long, I was angry and bitter with my daddy for not being the father I needed him to be. Life was about choices, right? So, why couldn't he choose his family? Time and time again, he failed me. I had to take care of him versus him take care of me which is not how it's supposed to be, right? I'd see my friends with their fathers, so close and happy. They could depend on their daddies to supply all their needs. I didn't even know what that looked like anymore. It was strange to watch. I longed for that relationship.

What I learned as I grew in the Lord is that what I needed and wanted from my daddy was something he wasn't capable of giving or being. His addictions and problems hindered his ability to be the daddy I wanted him to be. He was giving me all he was capable of giving.

Just because "I" was strong enough to fight addictions and "I" would never lose control over my life as he did, didn't mean my daddy had the same strength. He didn't and we, as hopeful humans, think others should have our abilities, our beliefs, our strengths, our goals, etc. But they don't and we can't "will" those qualities into someone...no matter how hard we try.

Accepting this reality and praying is all we can do, and then still, change may not come. But I (we) can give it to God! Recognize that we can't always fix it. God doesn't want us carrying the burdens alone. He will carry them for us.

Psalm 68:19 *Praise be to the Lord, to God our Savior, who daily, bears our burdens. NIV*

My daddy grew up in church. He was taught right from wrong, and he believed in God. God resided in his heart, but his addictions and demons overtook the majority of the space in his heart and his life. My daddy, alone, wasn't able...he wasn't strong enough to move those demons out. So his life was hard, to say the least. He could never crawl out of his dark hole.

There is a direct correlation between how much space God has in your heart and how your life turns out. Don't get me wrong, people with God in the forefront still have struggles. They still hurt. They still suffer loss, BUT they have God to lean on and carry them through. There is a peace with God.

My daddy didn't have that peace because God wasn't first in his life. In the end though – WOW! – God came to the forefront JUST IN TIME!

August 1, 2014 – **Obeying God**

This particular summer, I spent most of my weekends at the river with my family. My mama and stepdad have a trailer within walking distance of the beautiful shore. As I'd sit on the end of the pier watching the kids play, the Lord would often speak into my spirit.

There are times in our life when God will speak to us. He will speak to us through different means. In my case, the Holy Spirit placed a thought in my mind, a feeling in my heart, an urgency in my soul. When we experience one of the above, it is our choice to obey or ignore. Obedience to God's commands is the true sign of your love for God.

1 Samuel 15:22 *Does the Lord delight in burnt offerings and sacrifices as much as in obeying the Lord? To obey is better than sacrifice, and to heed is better than the fat of rams. NIV*

I look back on my life and ask, "Could I have done more?"...More to help Daddy, more to help others get saved, more for the glory of God?! The answer for all of us is yes! There is always more we could do. First, we have to listen to God, and if you have doubts that it is him, pray! Pray for discernment to know that it IS God. Next, we have to obey. Part of obeying is taking action.

This book would have never been written if I had not obeyed God. Only GOD knows who this book will help. It could be one or one hundred. The night Daddy died, a social worker called to get me to the hospital. The Holy Spirit convicted me to turn around to talk with Daddy about his salvation. If I hadn't listened, obeyed and acted, my daddy might be in hell right now!

The Holy Spirit has convicted me on countless occasions in my life, and I have ignored him many times. I have ignored God, which is disobedience to him. I prolonged my salvation for years and put myself at risk of going to hell. I hate to even think about times I may have ignored God that resulted in a lost soul remaining lost or even a lost soul going to hell.

When God speaks to us and convicts us to do something, I know it may seem hard, unthinkable, impossible or just undesirable. It is usually because we have to give up something, work harder, or start doing something new. Whatever the case, just know God will help you do it. You may not know who it is helping, but know that God is in control!

August 7, 2014 – **Unconditional Love**

As I continued to write, I had to somewhat relive my past. It brought back so many different emotions and made me realize just how difficult it is to love unconditionally…then and now!

As a young child, my daddy would scare me by yelling. He would even threaten to kill us. I loved him unconditionally, though, no matter what he did. That is a Godly love we should all have for one another, no matter what our faults.

As a teenager and young adult, Daddy's tactics affected me in a different way. His actions and his words made me bitter, angry. There were times when I hated him and everything he stood for. I struggled with these emotions for years. That childlike, Godly love wasn't in me.

Through it all, somehow I never left him. I never turned my back on him. I felt an obligation to him. He was my daddy! But most times, I resented every minute of it.

As I grew spiritually, learning from the Bible and from leaders in my church, I gradually got back to the childlike, Godly love, I had for Daddy so long ago. I loved him in my own way as a child of God – ***Unconditionally!***

August 18, 2014 – **Lean on God**

Writing about Daddy's chaotic behavior put me right back on the roller coaster ride I said I'd never get on again. I remembered how difficult it was to ask for God's help because I thought I could fix everything alone. I was so wrong!

I was so very weak when it came to handling my daddy's problems, his alcoholism, and everything that came with it. I was so overwhelmed. Sometimes I felt like the only person in the world going through this. I felt so alone, but I wasn't!

While I was failing miserably at dealing with Daddy's problems, I was failing even more at leaning on God. Why do we try to come up with all the answers when God has them all?

Sometimes God allows us to experience the "bad," the "hard," and the "lonely," to help us call on him. When we finally do, it all becomes so clear. If only I had done it sooner!

Throughout Daddy's life, I know he called on God, and God was there. Daddy's addictions paralyzed him, though. I don't know if it was his guilt or depression, but Daddy just didn't want to be helped… by me, God, or anyone.

Daddy finally "leaned on God" when it counted the most!

August 26, 2014 – **The Power of Afflictions**

So, I was back at the river writing about the last few years of Daddy's life. The writing had exhausted me both mentally and physically, but ironically enough, all I could think about was how it all ended – the glory and the triumph.

When you are looking back on life – a life filled with afflictions, pain, burdens, and grief – isn't it hard to ever feel like there was any good? Even when we are going through difficult times now, it is almost impossible to be positive, to see the light at the end of the tunnel. Ernest directed me to a powerful Scripture.

2 Corinthians 4:17 For this light momentary affliction is preparing for us an eternal weight of glory beyond all comparison. ESV

The afflictions made me who I am today, BUT only by the grace of God! He can help us see clearly when the trials and tribulations become blinding. Unfortunately, not until we see the end result do we finally believe! You would think we would learn by now to trust him in the storm.

All the afflictions of the past were nothing in comparison to the glory of Daddy's salvation!

August 30, 2014 – **Don't Enable, Set Boundaries**

You know, it took a long time for me to realize I was enabling Daddy. As I wrote about everything I did for him, it became so apparent right from the start. Why couldn't I see it then? I just had no control when it came to him – no control over my mouth, my emotions, nothing!

Ephesians 6:2-4 *Honor your father and mother – which is the first commandment with a promise –*

So that it may go well with you and that you may enjoy long life on the earth.

Fathers, do not exasperate your children; instead, bring them up in the training and instruction of the Lord.

These are the verses that resonated through my spirit every time Daddy and I had an argument. It was so easy to fly off the handle when he called to make me aware of his reckless behavior. It could be a call from jail to bail him out or a call to let me know he didn't have the money to pay his rent. As soon as the argument ended, I immediately felt badly and asked for forgiveness for disrespecting my daddy. I would laughingly say, "But God, he provoked my anger." I knew it didn't work that way.

For countless years, I unknowingly enabled my daddy. I allowed myself to be sucked into his addiction. I thought I was helping him. I was trying to fix him, but little did I know my help was hurting him and me. I didn't know where to draw the line. He always wanted me to pick up the pieces, and I didn't know how to say no. I fussed, yelled and expressed my utmost dislike of Daddy's behavior. Sometimes, I felt like God was punishing me.

With God's help, though, I was able to control my tongue and control the situation by setting boundaries. God showed me that I needed boundaries in my relationship with Daddy in order to have a healthy relationship. In the Bible, Jesus set boundaries even when he was helping others. He didn't always say "yes."

Once I understood this, things changed. Daddy knew that with me there to pick up the pieces, he could live irresponsibly...recklessly. I had to learn that saying no was okay. Once I started, to my amazement, Daddy was okay. I used to think if I didn't help him, he wouldn't survive, but he did. I didn't cut Daddy off completely, but I put restrictions on my contact with him. I visited periodically. We talked on the phone once a week, but the contact was on my terms. If I didn't like the conversation, I respectfully ended it. Thankfully, God also took burdens off my shoulders once I set boundaries – once I obeyed him.

Setting boundaries helped me retain my identity and helped me to heal! Boundaries saved my relationship with Daddy. It helped me keep my sanity and turned a destructive relationship into one I could live with – a relationship where I could honor my father – both of them!

September 5, 2014 – **Do It for God's Glory**

I was actually at work when the Lord led me to write this next passage. I was thinking about life, Daddy, our purpose here on earth, and why we do the things we do.

Through all the years of trying to help Daddy, there were times I felt like a stranger would have been more appreciative. No matter what I did, it was never enough. I felt taken for granted on so many occasions.

God helped me realize that Daddy's addictions caused him to be selfish and blind to what was important in life. All he could do was want more and not appreciate what he was already getting. Most importantly, though, God showed me what I was doing for Daddy wasn't for me. It wasn't for Daddy. It was for God's glory.

Everything we do in this life should be for the glory of God. Whether we are helping a family member with addictions, doing our best work at our daily job, or serving in our church, it should be done for the glory of God.

So if you don't get the "thank you" or the pat on the back you're looking for, just know God is smiling down on you when your efforts are for his glory.

September 13, 2014 – **Keep Praying**

There were times during the writing process I felt so ashamed. I was so ashamed of how I felt about Daddy back then. I had thrown in the towel and just knew God had as well. If only we were like God and able to hate the sin and not the sinner. It was hard for me to differentiate!

Do you have someone in your life who knows how to press all your buttons, get under your skin, or bring you down as low as them?

My daddy was that person for me. Even though he is now gone, I still have people in my life that affect me this way. I suppose we all do.

There were times in my life when I prayed for change in my daddy, and sadly, there were times when I didn't pray for him at all because I didn't think he deserved my prayers. I knew God had closed the door on him. It is hard to be compassionate when someone treats you so badly.

However, it is our job as Christians to rise above this. I learned, with God's help, those people that are so hard to pray for are the ones that need it the most. They are scared, guilt-ridden, and in desperate need of the Lord. We can help them get there with the Lord's guidance.

The year before Daddy died, I prayed for a miracle. I told God I was pretty sure he would be the one to change my daddy. I had finally accepted I couldn't do it. I am so glad I didn't stop praying. A miracle is certainly what God delivered.

2 Peter 3:9 *The Lord is not slow in keeping his promise, as some understand slowness. Instead, he is patient with you, not wanting anyone to perish, but everyone to come to repentance. NIV*

September 22, 2014 – **Carrying Others' Burdens**

I don't know about you, but I have a "type A" personality. There's not a challenge too great, so I thought. With Daddy, I knew I took on too much, but not until I laid everything out on paper in this book, did I realize just how much. It was a true eye-opener.

Carrying Daddy's burdens for so many years was my choice, but it came with great consequences. Throughout my life, being that "fix it" kind of person unintentionally caused me to carry loads I didn't have to carry. I laugh now thinking of all the times I prayed to God, but never really asked for his help. I've always believed God has blessed me so much, and I am so thankful. I don't want to complain or burden him with "my stuff." I can handle it, and I'll just pray God will help "me" fix the problem. I had it so wrong!

By doing this – by making it all my burden – I became numb. My heart became cold, and at times I felt I had lost all feeling for my daddy. There were times I could hardly recognize him. I didn't know the man I called "Daddy" anymore.

We have to recognize the difference between burdens that are okay for us to carry and burdens that are meant for God to carry. I should have given those burdens to God a lot sooner. The Lord wants us to help others by getting involved, helping that person get back to where they once were and most importantly, doing it with love. If we lose the love, then God is not a part of it, and we have to let him be! We have to lessen the load before it buries us and our emotions.

Psalm 55:22 *Cast your cares on the Lord and he will sustain you; He will never let the righteous be shaken. NIV*

Thankfully, God helped me lessen the load before Daddy died. By doing so, in Daddy's last hour, love was resurrected in the hearts of my daddy and me. That love allowed me one last glimpse of the daddy I knew so long ago. Most importantly, God's love filled Daddy's heart so his salvation could be claimed!

October 1, 2014 – **Love Harder, Speak Softer**

This particular day wasn't one of my best days. Do you have those days when everything goes the opposite way you need it to go? I found myself raising my voice at the ones I love most, my husband and daughter. As I worked on the book that day, I remembered how I yelled at Daddy on so many occasions…how we both said such hurtful things to one another.

Don't let the stresses of this life cause us to treat the people we love badly. It isn't always what we say but how we say it.

When Daddy was going through some of his worst years of addiction and self-destruction, our conversations were filled with hurtful words toward one another. We argued, yelled and disrespected each other. I let his behavior stress me to the highest degree. Of course, you know, no one but "I" was going through a stressful situation with her alcoholic daddy. We tend to feel like we're the only ones, but we aren't. I allowed Daddy to dictate my behavior. I used to actually blame him for how I talked and acted toward him.

Not until I realized it was me with the problem could I start to change. No matter what my daddy said or did – no matter what anyone says or does – as a Christian, I choose my response. I choose my words. Life can get us down, but God can help us handle it if we only ask. Words are hard to take back once said.

We should not live in fear of dying or worry everyday something bad is going to happen, but be aware that at anytime, your loved one may leave this world. God showed me the error of my ways well before Daddy died. Thank goodness!! I don't think I could live with myself if we had argued and then God had taken him before I could say, "I'm sorry Daddy." Living our lives with that simple thought tucked away in our minds should be sobering enough to keep us all in check. No matter how justified we think we are or how provoked, speak as Jesus did…love as he did. If we remember that, then we will love harder and speak softer!

Ephesians 4:29	*Don't let any unwholesome talk come out of your mouths, but only what is helpful for building others up according to their needs, that it may benefit those who listen. NIV*
Matthew 15:11	*What goes into someone's mouth does not defile them, but what comes out of their mouth, that is what defiles them. NIV*

November 7, 2014 – **Compassion**

I've always thought of myself as a compassionate person. Overall, I genuinely love and care for people. This book slapped me in the face, though, and showed me how uncompassionate I was when it came to Daddy. Now, most people would say I was justified, but are we really?

Compassion…what does it mean? It means sympathetic concern for the sufferings and misfortunes of others, to have mercy. This definition doesn't stipulate how the misfortunes occurred or whose fault it was that they occurred. We do that. I guess we feel if someone gets himself into a bind, he doesn't deserve compassion or mercy.

I struggled with this throughout life with my daddy. Every time he had a wreck, got robbed, lost money or whatever misfortune he suffered, it was so hard to have compassion because I felt like he did it to himself.

Is that fair? What if God did that to us? – Only gave mercy to the ones who didn't make bad decisions, ones that didn't make mistakes? He wouldn't feel much compassion or have mercy on any of us! Think about it. Don't let your compassion be conditional.

Ephesians 4:32 *Be kind and compassionate to one another, forgiving each other, just as in Christ God forgave you. NIV*

Forgiveness

I once read, "Forgive people in your life, even those who are not sorry for their actions. Holding on to anger only hurts you, not them." As I read this, I could only think about Daddy and how hard it was to forgive him over and over again.

Matthew 6:14	*For if you forgive other people when they sin against you, your Heavenly Father will also forgive you. NIV*

Webster's dictionary defines forgiveness as the act of forgiving, giving up resentment toward an offender, letting go of anger toward someone.

As a teenager and young adult, I resented Daddy. I had nothing but bitterness in my heart for him. Forgiveness was not in me at that time.

As I grew in the Lord and became a more mature adult, my heart matured. I looked at where I was in life, how blessed I was, and I thanked God. I thanked God for my entire life – the good and all the bad. It was all for a reason, a purpose...God's purpose. At that point, I was able to forgive Daddy for my childhood and for everything he couldn't be.

But...what do you do when the offender keeps offending? In Daddy's last ten years, we had new struggles. Through the disappointment, the using and abusing, the continued verbal abuse, I was faced daily with feelings of anger, resentment, and bitterness. You can say that you forgive and forget, but you can't forget especially when it hits you in the face day after day.

This was a major obstacle for me because it was so important to me to live my life as a Christian and abide by God's commandments. I didn't want my struggles with Daddy to send me to hell. I wanted to handle this situation as God would. It was so hard, though. I prayed, and I made mistakes, but God was there through it all. I felt a little beaten and bruised, but I didn't ever turn my back on Daddy. I was there to help, and gave what I could. Yes, I had to forgive the unforgivable. I was constantly forgiving the same things over and over. It actually got to a point when Daddy called with a dilemma, I laughed. I'd shake my head and just work through it with God by my side. Ernest once said, "You know you've really forgiven someone when you can laugh in the face of adversity…you no longer let the anger and resentment take over."

In that last hour on December 22, 2013, I don't think God would've allowed me the honor of leading Daddy to him if forgiveness wasn't in my heart. Forgiveness didn't only release me, but it helped release my daddy into the arms of the Lord.

Do you know how many times God forgives us for the same things over and over? There is someone out there you need to forgive. You may need to forgive yourself. Do it before it is too late. Free yourself and let God bless you. In turn, you may be able to bless others.

November 19, 2014 – **As Sheep, We Go Astray**

Just when I thought I was done with this book, the Lord added this chapter. It is amazing the way he works in our lives. I am in awe when I see what he has done for my family and me.

My daughter, Tori, is five years old. While writing this book, I never sat her down and told her what I was doing. However, she heard me discussing the book many times. She knew it was about her granddaddy. You never think they are paying attention until one day, they amaze you.

Tori participates in the AWANA program at Parker's Chapel every Wednesday night. It is Christian-based learning and fun for children of all ages. We have activities each week to complete with Scriptures to memorize. Her Scriptures this particular week were:

John 10:27	*My sheep hear my voice, and I know them, and they follow me. KJV*
Isaiah 53:6	*All we like sheep have gone astray; we have turned everyone to his own way…KJV*

My husband was reading the stories to her that correlated with the Scriptures. There are fictional stories, real life stories, and biblical stories to help her relate in every way possible. My husband began to read, "In the Bible, Jesus says he is the Good Shepherd. Like a shepherd loves each sheep, Jesus loves each one of us. But sometimes we are like sheep who don't listen to Jesus, our Shepherd. We go astray, which means we sin and do what we want instead of obeying what Jesus tells us to do in the Bible."

While we were reading and talking through the activities, Tori was also looking at the television...partly our fault. We actually turned it off at one point, but she kept reassuring us, "I got it mommy," as her eyes kept moving from us to the television screen.

When we were finished, though, I was astounded by what I heard. She leaned in toward me and whispered, "Mommy, I have to tell you something." Of course, I said, "Ok, tell me." She wanted to whisper it in my ear for whatever reason, so I leaned in. She whispered, "Does that (our AWANA lesson) make you think about your book?" I moved back and asked, "What did you say?" She said, "Does the sheep make you think about your book?" I smiled and said, "Yes, baby, it makes me think about the book."

I thought about what she said all night and into the morning. It hit me getting dressed the next morning. My daddy was a lost sheep. His sin caused him to go astray. He knew his shepherd's voice, but the voice was muffled by his addictions. Jesus never gave up on looking for his sheep, though. In the end, no matter how far my daddy wandered, Jesus eventually found him.

The Bible records many instances where God used one individual to deliver a message to others. He can use a friend, a parent, a pastor, or even a child. God entrusted MY child to deliver a message to me. What an awesome God!

December 13, 2014 – **God's Grace**

Isn't it funny? The Lord waited until the very end to give me a simple, but important message. Grace is what came…Just in Time!

Through the journey of writing this book, God revealed so much to me. He showed me this story isn't about Daddy's struggle or mine. It isn't just about the night Daddy died. This book is about God's amazing grace…The grace he gave over and over again throughout my life and throughout Daddy's life. This is the same grace he gives to all of us.

What is grace exactly? Is it the favor of God shown to the good, the Christian, the deserving? Justin Holcomb explains it best when he said, "Grace is the most important concept in the Bible, Christianity, and the whole world. Grace is the love of God shown to the unlovely; the peace of God given to the restless; the unmerited favor of God."

God's grace is NOT conditional. There is nothing we can do to earn it. It is granted to the righteous Christian, but also to the undeserving sinner. God grants his grace to us for no other reason than because he loves us! Don't ever forget that God loves you!

Song Inspired by the Lord – **Just in Time, God's Grace**

The night the Lord gave me the title of the book, *Just in Time*, He also gave me this song. The Lord flooded my mind with so much that night. I literally ran downstairs and wrote the two verses in less than thirty minutes. I knew this was a "God thing" because it definitely wasn't me. The chorus and bridge came later. Unfortunately, I don't read or write music…notes, that is. I have actually played around with a melody for the chorus and bridge, but I know God is going to do big things with this song to help inspire others. I am waiting and praying for his will to be done.

Verse 1…

He'd been there so many times before.
Frail and weak,
We had always wanted more.

For his life, we prayed
The Lord would guide

His heart up to the heavens
Before the day he died.

As I said, "I'm here, I love you dad,"
His last breath he'd soon take.
I heard the Lord say to me
"This is the step I need you to make."

Verse 2…

I turned around,
Whispered in his ear,
"I know you believe
And I need to hear."

He nodded "Yes,"
And, together, we prayed;
His sins would be forgiven;
This is the path the Lord had made.

On this night
The Lord put everything in place.
On this night
God Almighty gave us grace!

Chorus…

God's grace
God's grace….Came just in time

All the struggles,
All the trials…
What a mountain to climb!

When I was weak, you were strong –
How did everything go wrong?
It was his grace,
God's grace…Came just in time!

Bridge…

Lord, I thought that you had closed the door.
For so long, he told you, "No!"
But tonight would be his final chance…
Would he stay or would he go?

Then I felt your Spirit fill the place,
And I heard you from your throne,
"I am here to take my son! –
I am here to take him home!"

AUTHOR'S NOTE

I want everyone to know I struggled writing this book. I was truly excited to tell how God's grace came "*Just in Time*" to save my daddy. I was even more excited about inspiring and helping others better cope with family members who had addictions. I wanted to obey God. However, I would have to share some pretty harsh things about my daddy. I did NOT want to dishonor his memory or his life.

I hope I have depicted the many good qualities Daddy had. These were "my" experiences and "my" memories. Others may have different views about my daddy's life, but in the end, God's work was done. I had to paint the picture of the addict, the lost soul, the father whose struggles were real! His demons and his choices caused him to do, act, and say things that were unthinkable. But even after all that, God still welcomed him with open arms! Others experiencing this needed to see the severity of our situation to be able to relate. I hope you'll see the victory as well.

God has an audience this book is meant to reach. I pray it blesses, reassures and gives hope to you all. Most importantly, I hope souls are saved and relationships are mended before it is too late.

This is only a small step for me in serving the Lord, and I can't wait for him to direct my next steps. God bless you all!

ACKNOWLEDGEMENTS

I have so many to thank for helping me on this journey. I am so grateful to God almighty for entrusting me with this great honor and for surrounding me with wonderful people to help make *Just in Time* a reality.

My family has been my rock. Thank you, Dexter and Tori, for your sacrifice and encouragement. I want to thank my mama, sister, aunts, and cousins for helping me capture the past. Jazett Shivers, words cannot express how grateful I am for your guidance, your time, and your inspiration. I can't forget those co-workers who listened so diligently and offered words of advice. I am sure there is a word, a comma, or something in this book that is because of you. Ernest Silver, my mentor and brother in Christ, your wisdom has been invaluable. Thanks for keeping me grounded. Pastor Gene Williams and Pastor Wayne Flora, the words of your sermons penetrated hearts and won souls for the glory of the Lord. I thank you! Pastor Wayne and Lou Flora, the love and time you both put into helping edit *Just in Time* was truly a gift from God. I will never be able to thank you enough! Also, thanks to all the staff at Westbow Press. With your help, *Just in Time* is going to change lives.

Last but not least, I want to thank my daddy for being all he could be. See you in heaven!